THE BEST OF

jazz

THE BEST OF

jazz

The Essential CD Guide

Martin Gayford

CollinsPublishersSanFrancisco
A Division of HarperCollins*Publishers*

First published in the United States in 1993 by Collins Publishers San Francisco, 1160 Battery Street, San Francisco, California 94111

Text and Design copyright © 1993 by Carlton Books Limited, London
CD Guide format copyright © 1993 Carlton Books Limited
The Essential CD Guides is a registered trademark

Library of Congress Cataloging-in-Publication Data

Gayford, Martin. 1952-
The best of jazz : the essential CD guide / Martin Gayford.
   p. cm. — (The Essential CD guides)
Discography: p.
Includes index.
ISBN 0-00-255339-2
1. Jazz musicians—Biography—Dictionaries. 2. Jazz—History and criticism. 3. Compact discs—Reviews. I. Title. II. Series.
ML 102.J3G4 1993
781.65—dc20
                        93-11541
                            CIP
                            MN

Printed in Great Britain

THE AUTHOR
Martin Gayford writes on jazz for the British newspapers *The Spectator* and *The Daily Telegraph*.

Contents

INTRODUCTION

The sound of the Twentieth Century

N THE EARLY SEVENTIES, AN INTEREST IN JAZZ WAS ECCENTRIC INDEED. EVEN NOW, DESPITE RADIO STATIONS DEVOTED EXCLUSIVELY TO IT, FEATURE FILMS DWELLING ON ITS HEROES, AND ALL SORTS OF UNPRECEDENTED MEDIA HULLABALOO, MANY PEOPLE, THOUGH INTERESTED, REMAIN UNCLEAR AS TO EXACTLY WHAT JAZZ IS.

Actually, since it was first (rather disapprovingly) detected in the seedier areas of New Orleans around the time of the First World War, jazz has ramified and developed at such a dizzy rate that water-tight definition is an impossibility. It would be safe, however, to say that jazz is an improvised and syncopated music that emerged in America from a tangled mass of roots in African music plus European classical, tin-pan alley and folk.

How did this momentous fusion come about? Jazz, like its musical cousins and brethren, owes its existence to a terrible uprooting—the transportation of millions of African slaves across the Atlantic to work in the plantations of the New World. With them the survivors of the middle passage brought, often as their sole possession, the African culture hidden within their heads. And of that culture, music was an extremely important part. Those African slaves had a musical tradition of equal sophistication to that of the West, but

one which had developed in a diametrically opposite direction. Where Europeans had focused on harmony, with equivalent zeal Africans had concentrated on an aspect of music which remained rudimentary in the European system: rhythm. There were other differences too, including a less formal style of performance and an openness to participation from the audience. All left traces in the characteristic informal mood of jazz in club and bar.

But almost as soon as they arrived, these Afro-Americans started to blend their native traditions with the existing European forms. By and by, their white compatriots began to take an interest in the fascinating and exciting black music that emerged as a result.

Jazz has produced many figures—Louis Armstrong, Duke Ellington, Charlie Parker and John Coltrane among them—who are important musicians by any standards. Their sounds are all around us in other music. The influence of jazz, though not always acknowledged, has been all-pervasive.

Jazz is uniquely a music of our age in its dynamism, its mixed cultural roots and the astonishing speed of its evolution. Its birth more or less coincided with the dawn of the twentieth century—according to the most plausible guess, it was very soon after 1900 that a few adventurous musicians in New Orleans began to play in a new idiom, brasher, freer, more dynamic and more exciting than ragtime. So it's fairly safe to say that, as the rest of the world embarks on the twenty-first century, jazz will be celebrating its first 100 years.

But the music itself has often seemed a trifle esoteric to the general public. These days the sheer range and choice of recordings available under the heading "jazz" is astonishingly—bewilderingly—vast. In 1993 more is about on CD than ever there was on vinyl. So much indeed that compiling a brief guide such as this is a daunting, and potentially risky, task.

The criteria for selecting 100 significant musicians, 10 legends and 20 landmark albums are bound to be personal and to some extent arbitrary. The choice no doubt reflects my own predilection for tradition-al, mainstream and bebop, and my judgement that these styles represent the historical core of the music. If few of the players and recordings discussed come from outside America, that is not because much excellent music has not been made elsewhere. It has. It is because in a book of this kind it seemed best to concentrate on the major innovators, and they—with a few exceptions like Django Reinhardt—have all been American. Several significant European figures of the last two decades—Jan Garbarek and John McLaughlin, for example—perform in an idiom so far from the basic jazz line that they seem to belong more comfortably in a book about improvised music. The question, "What is jazz?" is certainly getting more difficult all the time.

Even taking a rigorously restrictive view of jazz has meant making some hard choices. Several of my favourite musicians—the trumpeter Hot Lips Page, for example—ended up being excluded. The selection of the 20 best jazz recordings was just as ticklish. My criteria here were twofold: first, whether the music in question is outstandingly good, and second, whether it is historically important. Sometimes a whole series of recordings seemed to qualify, like the Armstrong Hot Fives. On other occasions a single performance stood out, such as Hawkins's 'Body And Soul'. If the reader is wondering whether the fact that no fusion album is included reflects a prejudice of the author's, it does.

When buying jazz recordings, it is worth remembering that only material from the Fifties onwards was originally conceived for long-playing discs, and the earlier record-ings have appeared in various different compilations over the years. Most jazz recordings (including for-eign imports) are only readily avail-able in specialist shops, so they are not that easy to get hold of. However, persevere. Jazz is a vast field full of the most diverse vari-eties of excellent music and there are few things more worth listening to.

THE SOUND of NEW ORLEANS

The origin of Jazz

NEW ORLEANS IS AND WAS AN EXCEPTIONAL PLACE. ORIGINALLY A FRENCH SETTLEMENT, IT ONLY BECAME PART OF THE USA WITH THE LOUISIANA PURCHASE OF 1803. SITED ON THE BANKS OF THE MISSISSIPPI, IT LOOKED SOUTH TO LATIN AMERICA AND THE CARIBBEAN, HENCE THE ELEMENT IN NEW ORLEANS MUSIC WHICH JELLY ROLL MORTON DUBBED "THE SPANISH TINGE".

Throughout the nineteenth century, New Orleans retained a French-speaking upper class—the creoles—who looked to Paris for their culture. It was tough. The street parades—still an essential part of city life—might result in pitched battles between the inhabitants of rival areas. "If they'd have ten fights one Sunday," Jelly Roll Morton recounted, "they didn't have many."

No doubt the reality could be squalid; but with hindsight old-time New Orleans sounds wonderful. Street parades, Mardi Gras, picnics, dances, funerals, brothels—in the memories of those who lived through it, all of these merged into one enormous party.

the story of jazz

Consequently, there was a tremendous demand for one commodity—music. It was met largely by two groups: working-class blacks and creoles of colour. It is in the interaction between these two that many have seen the origin of jazz.

The creoles were craftsmen and small tradesmen—cigar-makers, shoemakers, tailors—and jealous of their status. They played with a conventional, "legitimate" technique.

As against the creoles' well-trained fluency, the black musicians had one great asset: the rhythmic flair which came from Africa. They didn't, and generally couldn't, read musical scores, but instead played "head music"—that is, by ear and memory. When they got to New Orleans, the black players took up the instruments of the creole bands—cornet, trombone, clarinet, tuba, bass. But at moments of emotional climax they continued to roughen their instrumental sounds as a gospel or blues singer would.

And, like an African drummer, they swung.

The exact sequence of events—who contributed what and when—we are never likely to know as no recordings were made of New Orleans jazz until 1917, and none of black or

creole musicians until several years after that. The first major player of whom we hear was a black barber and cornettist named Buddy Bolden (1877–1931), but Bolden made no records and was committed to a mental hospital in 1907, where he remained for the rest of his life. He was noted for his forceful sound and probably he remained closer to ragtime rhythm than to fully-fledged jazz.

The first jazz musicians of whom we have adequate recordings were born a little later. Most important among them were Joe "King" Oliver (1885–1938), Ferdinand "Jelly Roll" Morton (1890–1941), Sidney Bechet (1897–1959) and Louis Armstrong (1901–71), all of whom recorded, not in New Orleans, where there were no studios until later on, but in Chicago.

The cornet was the dominating instrument in New Orleans bands, the one around which the others pivoted. New Orleans jazz is an

Louis Armstrong, New Orleans' greatest player and the one who changed New Orleans jazz into a soloist's art.

ensemble music; from time to time one instrument comes to the fore, then another, but much of the time most of the musicians are playing.

The cornet would give the music its basic melodic direction, or as the players called it, its lead ("Play more lead on that cornet!" Oliver would tell his young protégé, Louis Armstrong). Above this, the clarinet would weave a fluid, higher part.

The trombonists, of whom Kid Ory was the most respected, would fill in below in the choppy New Orleans style (known as tailgate, because when a band played on a cart, the trombonist had to sit

Sidney Bechet: most fiery and audacious of New Orleans reed-players, whether on clarinet or soprano saxophone.

facing rearwards so he could manipulate his slide over the back). The rhythm instruments were generally drums, tuba or string bass and perhaps a banjo—New Orleans produced some superb rhythm players in the drummers Zutty Singleton, Baby Dodds and Paul Barbarin, and excellent bassists in Pops Foster and Wellman Braud. The piano was a rarity, partly because it was impossible to carry on parades, picnics and other mobile festivities.

During the Thirties, the New Orleans style was forgotten, but at the end of the decade a small group of fans started listening to the old recordings. On the recommendation of Louis Armstrong, the cornettist Bunk Johnson (1879–1949), an erstwhile colleague of Buddy Bolden, was summoned from retirement, provided with a new pair of false teeth, and was soon performing and recording to great acclaim. This was the beginning of the New Orleans revival. In the wake of the New Orleans revival other hitherto unknown

players started touring and recording, among them the clarinettist George Lewis and the trombonist Jim Robinson. It was discovered that the semi-professional street music of New Orleans was still alive.

Soon, young white players were trying to emulate this pre-swing style which had been superseded by Armstrong, Hawkins and Ellington 20 years before. In terms of world-wide popularity, New Orleans, traditional or "trad" jazz was far more important than bop. By the early Fifties, it was a tremendous craze in America and Europe, especially with students and bohemians. In Europe, trad was the immediate forerunner of rock, and supplied many of the same danceable qualities. It is still played all over the world.

Today, in New Orleans itself there are still street bands and performances at Preservation Hall, but hope for the future must rest on eclectic younger musicians, like those in the Dirty Dozen and Rebirth Brass Band, who use the music of their native city as a basis for something new.

JAZZ in the TWENTIES

Chicago and New York

MOST OF THE VITAL DEVELOPMENTS WHICH OCCURRED IN JAZZ DURING THE TWENTIES TOOK PLACE IN TWO CITIES, CHICAGO AND NEW YORK. BOTH WERE CENTRES OF THE ENTERTAINMENT INDUSTRY AND BOTH WERE MAGNETS FOR THE BLACK IMMIGRANTS WHO WERE STREAMING OUT OF THE SOUTHERN STATES IN THE FIRST HALF OF THE CENTURY IN SEARCH OF A BETTER DEAL.

By the Twenties there was a black quarter in Chicago—the South Side—with a population of around 100,000 people, while New York's Harlem was already a sort of capital city for the black population of the USA. And in both Chicago and New York young white musicians were catching on to this novel black music—as they had in New Orleans—and were beginning to make their own contribution.

Chicago was the place where most of the classic recordings were made by New Orleans musicians like King Oliver, Louis Armstrong, Johnny Dodds, Baby Dodds, Freddie Keppard, Jelly Roll Morton and Jimmy Noone. To Chicago also came up-and-coming musicians from other parts of the country, such as the dazzling young pianist from Pittsburgh, Earl Hines, and young white musicians from all over the Midwest whose ears had been enchanted by jazz—the cornettist Bix Beiderbecke from Davenport, Iowa, guitarist Eddie Condon from Indiana, and the clarinettist Pee Wee Russell from Missouri.

There they met a native Chicagoan coterie who had all attended a single school—Austin High—and which included a number of important musicians including a brilliant drummer, Dave Tough, and an extraordinary clarinettist named Frankie Teschmacher.

Some of these youths had first been inspired by the recordings of the Original Dixieland Jazz Band (ODJB), a rather frenetic copy of New Orleans jazz. But they soon realized that it was the great black musicians who were the fountainhead

More than any other performer, Earl Hines was responsible for freeing jazz piano from ragtime and blues.

of the music, and consequently went to sit at the feet of King Oliver at the Royal Gardens, Johnny Dodds at Kelley's Stables and so forth.

Curiously, this white Chicagoan jazz did not turn out a carbon-copy of the sounds of these men. The feeling was different. New Orleans jazz was deeply relaxed. In comparison these middle-class white Chicagoans sounded individualist and anarchic, which was probably because that was what they were: middle class dropouts, bohemians. They were the kind of people from whose ranks jazz (and later rock) musicians and fans have so frequently been recruited.

Paradoxically, these iconoclasts turned out to be surprisingly conservative. It was white players like Muggsy Spanier who preserved the archaic styles of King Oliver and company. The bands of survivors gathered by Eddie Condon in the Fifties and Sixties were playing much as they had in the Twenties. And still, it should be added, making excellent music. In the music of men like clarinettist Kenny Davern, the tradition still thrives today.

By the end of the Twenties, most of the major musicians in Chicago, white and black, had moved on to seek their fortunes in New York. There they found some jazz developments that had been happening in the north-east. In New York jazz had also been taken up by white musicians, most of whom took their cue from the ODJB. In general the results were more sedate than in Chicago, but the guitarist Eddie Lang, violinist Joe Venuti and trombonist Miff Mole evolved a refined chamber jazz idiom.

A more important factor in the north-east, however, was the local school of advanced ragtime pianists which is known to history as 'stride'. The name comes from the powerful and technically demanding bass patterns which were the hallmark of the style. These consisted of alternating widely spaced chords and single notes, giving the impression that the pianist's left hand was striding vigorously up and down the keyboard. Like classic ragtimers, the stride pianists wrote elaborate compositions intended to dazzle audiences and subdue their rivals. But in performance these could be extended indefinitely into a semi-improvised sequence of "tricks", such as harmonic runs or riffs (repeated phrases), designed to build up momentum and display virtuosity.

The stride pianists were loners and dandies, inclined to silver-topped canes and elaborately pleated overcoats. When they met one another, a gladitorial battle of music was likely to result, as might happen at the private, fund-raising rent parties which Harlem dwellers would throw in their flats. Of the Harlem pianists, the most typical was James P. Johnson (1894–1955), the most idiosyncratic William Henry Joseph Bonaparte Bertholoff Smith, known as Willie "The Lion" (1897–1973), and the most famous, Thomas "Fats" Waller (1904–43).

Johnson's fiendishly difficult 'Carolina Shout' was the benchmark of stride—the piece young players had to master. But it was perhaps Waller, Johnson's pupil and close follower, who left the most irresistible examples of the genre.

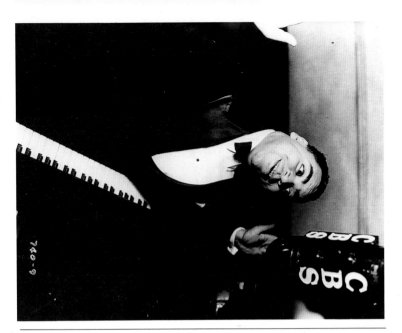

The irrepressible Fats Waller, inventor of the most irresistible examples of Harlem stride piano.

One more key event was happening in New York at this time. Various black musicians were finding ways in which to blend the freedom and improvisation of New Orleans jazz with the instrumentation of the kind of large ensemble that worked in New York dance halls and clubs. In other words, this was the birth of big band jazz.

The most brilliant musician in at the delivery was Duke Ellington, but his contribution was so individual that it had little influence in the short term. It was in the band led by Fletcher Henderson that the standard formula for big band arrangements was worked out. Saxophonist Don Redman carried out the groundwork. After his departure, the lazy Henderson continued, refining the division of the band into sections—trumpets, reeds, trombones—and simplifying what they played into riffs. The result was a big band that could play with the pared-down ease of a small group—the blueprint for the age of swing.

THE AGE of SWING

New York and Kansas City

Fletcher Henderson's band and arrangements provided the blueprint for the age of swing.

THE STORY OF JAZZ IN THE AGE OF SWING IS AGAIN LARGELY A TALE OF TWO CITIES: THIS TIME, NEW YORK AND KANSAS CITY. THE BIG APPLE BECAME MORE AND MORE THE MECCA FOR MUSICIANS FROM ALL OVER THE USA, AND HENCE THE CAPITAL OF THE JAZZ WORLD (WHICH IS MORE OR LESS WHAT IT HAS REMAINED EVER SINCE).

There were hundreds of jazz orchestras all over America in the Thirties—the so-called territory bands, many of which never recorded. But, sooner or later, most of the best bands and musicians ended up in New York. And it was there that most of the vital developments occurred.

By the early Thirties the major black bands working out of New York—Fletcher Henderson, Duke Ellington, Luis Russell, Cab Calloway—had become a sort of first division of the jazz world, gathering up most of the finest musicians in the country. These in turn set about inventing personal variations of the current idiom—basically, Louis Armstrong's—adapted to their own instrument. It was a fiercely competitive world, in which trumpeter would battle trumpeter, clarinettist challenge clarinettist, and so on, in after-hours clubs.

The object of the competition was to play higher or faster than the next guy, to improvise more inventively, or display a more beautiful tone. The best jobs went to those with something different to offer. Hence the characteristic variety of swing jazz. On every instrument in this era, it is possible to list half a dozen or more players, all more or less equally good and all offering a distinctive sound.

By the end of the decade—partly through this process of competition—the music itself had become faster, lighter, and built increasingly around repeated short phrases—riffs. This is the small-group swing sound that became associated with the more intimate clubs of New York, many of which were on 52nd Street—Swing Street. It is the style characteristic of small bands like the John Kirby Orchestra, the Benny

Goodman Sextet, the various little groups drawn from the Ellington and Basie bands, and the recording sessions made under the names of Lionel Hampton, Billie Holiday and Teddy Wilson.

In the late Thirties and Forties, the New York jazz scene was enriched by a regional invasion from the South-West, a huge swathe of land stretching down from the Great Plains into Texas—blues territory. This area had been full of musical activity since the Twenties, although many of the South-Western bands were not recorded well. Music thrived, especially in Kansas City, a wide-open gangster-run town where the clubs and bars never closed, and musicians never lacked for work.

The common factor in Kansas City music was the blues. Texan and South-Western

Born in Louisiana and raised in Texas, Illinois Jacquet was one of the great tenor saxophonists to come out of the South-West.

tenor saxophonists like Herschel Evans, Buddy Tate, Arnett Cobb, Illinois Jacquet and Budd Johnson had a natural way with them that northern musicians could seldom rival.

Also they swung with an easy lope that was freer and more insistent than jazz rhythm had been before.

Both characteristics were shown to perfection by the Count Basie Band when it descended on New York in 1937. The Basie rhythm section had perfected an india-rubber 4/4 beat which arguably swings as much as anything that has been heard before or since.

This was partly the result of the lightness and *élan* of the drummer, Jo Jones, partly the tact of Basie himself in paring down the piano contribution to the bare essentials, partly the unanimity of the bassist Walter Page and guitarist Freddie Greene in putting wheels under every beat. Less is more, was the lesson of Basie and Kansas City. In fact the whole band swung as never before on blues-based arrangements even simpler and more infectious than those of Fletcher Henderson. Most of these were "heads", made up collectively by the band. Many of the most important musicians of the next few years—Lester Young, Charlie Parker, Charlie Christian—came from the South-West.

Meanwhile, swing in another sense had conquered the world. Armed with Fletcher Henderson's conception of the big band, and many of Henderson's actual arrangements, the white band led by Benny Goodman became a national sensation in 1935. In the next few years big band swing became the dominant pop music of the world, and the leading bandleaders—Goodman, Artie Shaw, Tommy Dorsey—the stars of the day.

Most of them mixed more or less schmaltz with their jazz. Many, certainly the ones listed above, were capable of producing absolutely outstanding music from time to time, although perhaps only the finest black bands, Ellington and Basie in particular, consistently turned out truly great jazz. But the big bands were invaluable training-grounds both for listeners and musicians. It was in the big bands that generations of jazz musicians received their musical education.

The big-band craze was over by the mid-Forties, but that was by no means the end of swing jazz. The swing survivors were submerged by the fashions for bop and cool, but re-emerged in the late Fifties, their music rechristened mainstream. At this stage, men like Coleman Hawkins, Henry Red Allen and Pee Wee Russell did much of their finest work. Many swing veterans, Buddy Tate and the trombonist Vic Dickenson, for example, were playing superbly in the Seventies. A few major figures, notably the trumpeter Doc Cheatham and altoist Benny Carter, still perform regularly today. And over the years, they have been joined by a steady stream of recruits to the idiom including the cornetist Ruby Braff and tenor player Scott Hamilton. In the Eighties, a splendid mainstream band appeared in New York led by two musicians in their thirties, Dan Barrett and Howard Alden. All in all, the swing style has proved remarkably durable.

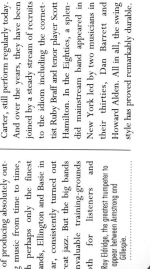

Roy Eldridge, the greatest trumpeter to appear between Armstrong and Gillespie.

THE SOUND of BEBOP

Jazz Revolution

B EBOP, THE JAZZ INSURRECTION OF THE FORTIES, WAS THE FIRST JAZZ STYLE TO COME ALONG SINCE LOUIS ARMSTRONG THAT WAS IN EVERY RESPECT NEW AND DIFFERENT. IT WAS ALMOST AS IF THE INVENTORS OF BOP HAD SAT DOWN AND SAID TO THEMSELVES "IS THAT HOW THE OLDER GUYS PLAY? WELL, WE'RE GOING TO DO IT THE OTHER WAY ROUND."

The difference between bop and swing is often seen as an harmonic question, a switch from diatonic to chromatic harmony. But there were other changes just as fundamental, notably a quickening of the pulse of jazz. Bop players loved quicksilver runs, and were fond of doubling the tempo even when playing ballads. Much of the most characteristic bop, however, was played at an astonishing, unprecedented pace. "That horn ain't *spos'd* to sound that fast" the swing tenor saxophonist Ben Webster is said to have declared on first hearing Charlie Parker's playing.

Bop musicians also did away with the polished instrumental tones of the swing era. Growls, smears and tonal effects were out. Gillespie, for example, built on Roy Eldridge's phenomenal ability to play high and fast on the trumpet; in time he played higher and faster than his model, on the edge of what is technically possible on the trumpet. And the stress in bop phrasing was often the

Dubbed "the high priest of bop," Thelonious Monk was in fact the new music's most original composer.

....

reverse of swing—on weak beats, not strong.

Altogether—strange harmonies, hell-for-leather speed, inverted phrasing, funny new instrumental tones—bop had an exotic sound to the conventional ear, hence the bandleader Cab Calloway's description of it as "Chinese music." Some of the older generation, like Hawkins and Young, played with boppers; but none could completely transfer to the style themselves. Bop was a watershed in jazz history.

The style was forged by the élite of younger black musicians; it was the music of a coterie, played in little clubs for people in the know. Later on it acquired a following, but it was never the dominant popular idiom of the Forties —that was provided by singers like Frank Sinatra. And the trappings of the bebop fans—the dark glasses, berets and goatee beards (imitated from Gillespie)—stressed that they were members of an esoteric inner circle. You needed to be knowledgeable to appreciate this complex, fiercely compressed music. With bop, jazz not only split into separate camps, it also split off from the broad mass of popular music. It became an art, a highbrow affair.

In 1939-41 the forerunners of bop liked to meet in two Harlem clubs, Minton's Playhouse and Monroe's Uptown House, with the leaders-to-be of the bop revolution, guitarist Charlie Christian, trumpeter Dizzy Gillespie, saxophonist Charlie Parker, pianist Thelonious Monk

and drummer Kenny Clarke. A few live recordings exist of sessions at Minton's and other Harlem clubs in 1940 and 1941.

Who contributed what to bop? Gillespie has insisted that it was a group effort. Kenny Clarke contributed the new drum idiom—keeping the rhythm in the cymbals while putting

the accent on the bass drum (the name bebop seems to have begun as an onomatopoeic way of describing a drum pattern). Thelonious Monk put in a lot of harmonic ideas, as did Gillespie himself. But Parker and Gillespie were seen as the leaders by musicians.

Of the two, Gillespie—the steadier character—was the one who rapidly became a famous name, the public face of bop. With his mischievous humour, his beard and beret he had an image as recognizable as Armstrong's handkerchief and grin. He conducted his career with the shrewdness and stamina of an Ellington or a Hampton ("Dizzy like a fox" someone once said of him). But wonderful though Dizzy was, Charlie Parker was the improvising genius. It was Parker who demonstrated the potential of the style with overwhelming power, as Armstrong had for swing.

The first full recording sessions by bop bands do not come until 1944 and 1945, by which time, especially in Parker's masterly tracks from the latter year, the music had been refined to perfection. By then, too, a number of important new figures had arrived. In the brilliant, psychologically unstable, pianist Bud Powell, the new music found its most influential keyboard performer.

A young drummer, Max Roach, applied the lessons of Kenny Clarke with more rhythmic freedom. J. J. Johnson attempted the difficult task of playing bop on the slide trombone. Milt Jackson did the same for the vibes. Two trumpeters, Fats Navarro and Miles Davis, appeared with less fiery, more reflective ways of playing than Gillespie.

Over the next few years the key bop records were made. Among the most important were Parker's on Savoy and Dial. Gillespie endeavoured to translate bop into big-band terms, While Tadd Dameron (with Navarro on trumpet) and Thelonious Monk made superb series of recordings which in different ways showed

The brilliantly lucid drumming of Max Roach is to be heard on many of Charlie Parker's best recordings.

how the music could be moulded by the sensibility of a composer.

By the late Forties, bop had swing on the run. Most of the younger generation of players were more or less marked by it, and in time bop became the basis of the modern jazz of the Fifties. Since then bop has had many rivals. But in the early Nineties, a full half century after those young revolutionaries met at Minton's, it is still more likely than not that an up-and-coming musician will take Parker, Gillespie or Bud Powell for a model.

Trumpeter Dizzy Gillespie was a major contributor to the new music and the first to organize a bop big band.

19

THE SOUND of COOL JAZZ

Take Five

As the dust settled from the bebop revolution of the forties, it turned out that, like most such events, it had been less thoroughgoing than it seemed at the time. Not only did swing survive as an idiom on its own, but many even of the younger generation included swing musicians as well as bop ones among their influences.

Between 1945 and 1955, most tenor saxophonists who came along were clones not of Charlie Parker, but of Lester Young, ex-star of the Count Basie band. Moreover, even while the bebops were conducting their experiments into rhythm and harmony, others were investigating musical areas like melody and structure. By the beginning of the Fifties, all these tendencies were grouped under a new label—the cool.

In part, this was a change of mood. Bop was furious, fast and hot; cool was less emotionally engaged, more melodic, lighter in feel. Among the key movers in the change was Miles Davis, a musician in the heart of the bop camp. Davis had been selected by Charlie Parker as his front-line partner in 1947–8, presumably because Davis's melodic middle-range approach was a perfect foil for Parker's own furioso.

But these interests led Davis towards a new conception of how a jazz ensemble could sound. He loved the Claude Thornhill band—an unorthodox white ensemble—whose sound, as Miles put it, "hung like a cloud". His idea was to take that mellow Thornhill style and apply it to a medium-sized group with a more out and out jazz policy. With some justification, the light, spry recordings of the Davis Nonet were later christened "The Birth of the Cool".

There was more to it than that, though. At this time, the influence of Lester Young was enormous on young tenor players, both black and white. Admittedly Lester himself was not exactly cool, but neither did he believe in laying emotion on with a bluesy or rhapsodic trowel. His followers tended to be a little more detached than Lester was himself, especially the white ones. Lester's musical children were fanatical in their devotion. "Anybody who doesn't play like Lester is wrong," one of them declared. They were also to be found all over the place. Dexter Gordon and Wardell Gray among the black players, and Allen Eager, Brew Moore, Stan Getz, Al Cohn and Zoot Sims among the white ones.

Another element in the mix that became the cool was provided by the reclusive pianist Lennie Tristano (1919–78). Tristano's principles might sound chilly, the reverse of warm, communicative jazz. He wanted musicians to play without tonal inflection, so that emotion came only from the line and structure of their solos—the areas in which he was an innovator. But in practice Tristano's music, though certainly intellectual in appeal, fizzes with new ideas. His influence was small at the time, but he has some affinity with the free jazz of the Sixties and Seventies. Indeed in 1949 a Tristano group was the first ever to record jazz without preset key, chords or melody.

There is a flirtation with classical music in a good deal of jazz of this time. It comes out in the preoccupation of the pianist Dave Brubeck, who had studied with Milhaud and Schoenberg, with devices such as counterpoint. In other ways his quartet, with its catchy tunes and brilliant, lighter-than-air altoist Paul Desmond, was hugely popular in the Fifties. More ponderously indigestible was the classicism of Stan Kenton, who once toured with Innovations In Modern Movement, a 40-piece band including a full string section. Kenton's music in fact was most classically innovatory and most traditionally jazzy. But the Kenton band was the nursery for a large number of musicians who subsequently settled in California and became associated with the notion of "West Coast Cool".

In reality, the idea that music in California was cooler than elsewhere was dubious. It was launched, in fact, by a story in *Life* magazine, and partly kept afloat by the James Dean looks of Chet Baker, trumpeter with the Gerry Mulligan Quartet. The laid-back sounds of Mulligan, Baker and some other white Californians fitted the beach boy image perfectly. Actually, the West Coast was a centre for much heated (black) bop. And some white Californians, like the altoist Art Pepper, were more impassioned than cool. But it was true that

Saxophonist Zoot Sims was among the most swinging and inventive of all the followers of Lester Young.

much gentle, lightly floating jazz was made by bands like Howard Rumsey's Lighthouse All Stars (resident in a club on Hermosa Beach) and Shorty Rogers Giants.

Cool jazz has come in for a great deal of criticism over the years for being feeble, insipid, unbluesy and white—charges in which there is some truth. The largely fictitious nature of the West Coast image did not help its reception either. But over the last decade people have come to appreciate that the various musicians who can loosely be described as cool produced a great deal of music which is on its own terms extremely enjoyable.

HARD BOP

Jazz in the Late Fifties

Like most art forms, jazz history is the result as much of swings from one fashion to another as of any logical progression from style to style. And by the mid Fifties, quite a lot of people were ready for an antidote to the rather languid sound of cool.

It came in the form of the reassertion of the heated bebop style, and of the African roots of jazz in blues and gospel. The result was sometimes labelled hard bop or funk, but these are names for a tendency rather than a separable style. Indeed a sceptic might say that nothing special began in the mid Fifties at all. A large number of musicians had continued to play, and develop, bebop throughout the era of the cool. All that occurred around 1955 was that record companies and journalists noticed them a bit more. But—though there is something in that—there was a change of emphasis between the first wave of bop and the music of the late Fifties.

The bop of the Forties was fairly esoteric stuff, more so in fact than the melodic and accessible cool. Parker, Powell and Gillespie played fast and furiously, and only the initiated could really follow them. Their heirs of the Fifties kept the heat, but added some simpler, more obviously enjoyable elements. The key transitional group here was the Clifford Brown–Max Roach Quintet which flourished between 1954 and Brown's death in 1956.

This was in many ways a lineal descendant of the original bop bands. Roach had been Charlie Parker's drummer in the mid Forties, Clifford Brown followed directly on from Dizzy Gillespie and Fats Navarro. But there was a subtle difference. Where Gillespie's playing was extreme in every way—faster and higher than previously seemed possible on the trumpet—Brown was basically calm and classical. He was middle-register player; many of his finest achievements were at medium tempo, or on ballads. His golden instrumental tone was as beautifully burnished as that of any swing musician. This was bop without a good deal of the fury.

Fury, or at any rate, a sort of aggressive assertiveness—expressed by a deliberately brusque tone—was present in the most important new tenor saxophonists John Coltrane and Sonny Rollins. But it was offset by other elements. In the Brown–Roach band the gruff Rollins acted as a foil to Clifford Brown's mellifluous trumpet. And even as a soloist he had some un-bop-like tendencies—

Trumpeter Clifford Brown, lost leader of Fifties jazz, plays with tenor saxophonist Sonny Rollins.

a liking for medium and ballad tempi, a way of improvising that didn't just throw away the initial theme, but built on it.

Drummers were becoming more and more noisy and important, none more so than Art Blakey, leader of the Jazz Messengers—the quintessential hard bop band. The Messengers were always a bebop group, grooming generation after generation of young musicians in the style. Again, however, it was bop

might be multi-noted and fierce-toned young lions like Jackie McLean or Johnny Griffin, but the band was pushed along by the tremendous shove of Blakey's drumming. And that was an element so powerful as to give the music a physically elating effect. Also, the Messengers went in for some very catchy themes—often derived in the late Fifties from fashionably earthy blues and gospel elements.

It is not clear who originated the back-to-the-gospel roots movement known as funk. Charlie Mingus later claimed he did with his churchy pieces 'Better Git It In Your Soul' and 'Wednesday Night Prayer Meeting'. But Horace Silver was first to record with his hummable theme 'The Preacher' (based on 'Show Me The Way To Go Home'). For a while, Silver specialized in funky pieces with his popular band— an outfit similar to the Messengers, with whom Silver had started out, but given its own character by Silver's

own compositions and spare, percussive piano-playing. Blakey recorded a number of examples of the genre—notably the hit 'Moanin'— while the bluesy pianist Bobby Timmons was in his band. The basic inspiration probably came from Ray Charles, whose appearance was one of the big musical events of the Fifties, but in the long run it was the altoist Cannonball Adderley who persisted longest with this bop plus blues and gospel mix, and gained the greatest popularity from it.

The appeal of funk or hard bop was connected with a new interest in black roots—a first stirring of the black power movement. It was also based on a deliberate search for popularity. The blues were and are one of the perennially crowd-pleasing ingredients in jazz. (Other manifestations of them at this time were organ jazz and the honking and hollering tenor and organ combos, like those led by Lockjaw Davis). Both impulses—black consciousness and the quest for popularity—played important parts in the next phases of the development of jazz.

FREEDOM

The New Thing

By the Fifties jazz had become habituated to messianic figures—"the leather-stockinged geniuses", the critic Gary Giddins once put it—who came along and taught the world a new musical language. Louis Armstrong, Lester Young, Charlie Parker... who would be next?

Was Ornette Coleman—an iconoclastic young altoist who had recently blown into New York from the West Coast—the new Bird? It seemed probable. He had extremely disturbing musical ideas, which defied conventional notions of harmony. His instrumental sound was raw, fresh and expressive in a novel way, just as Parker's had been. Previously, just like Parker and Lester Young, Coleman had been derided by older musicians, boppers like Dexter Gordon. He had many of the marks of a messiah. But the jazz world was divided. Many—including the normally avant-garde Miles Davis and Charles Mingus—were suspicious, openly suggesting that Coleman's playing showed not so much profound originality as profound ignorance.

But the radicality of Coleman's music suited the spirit of the times. It promised a great step forward—agreeable to the modern-minded Sixties—and it proposed a new type of music which would be more clearly the possession of black Americans. This had been one of the initial motives of bop. But that, of course, had been very quickly assimilated by white performers.

This new music—the New Thing, as it was sometimes called—was arguably a sort of return to more purely African roots, jettisoning the European elements in jazz: conventional harmony and form. And indeed, some of Coleman's work does indeed suggest the most primitive Afro-American blues and field hollers. By the beginning of the Sixties, a number of younger musicians were following Coleman's lead, including the tenor players Albert Ayler (1936–70) and Archie Shepp (b. 1937).

By the mid Sixties, John Coltrane himself—another putative messiah—had adopted free jazz. His major records of 1965 —*Ascension, Meditation, Kulu Se Mama*—were recorded with such collaborators as Shepp and an Albert Ayler follower called Pharoah Saunders (b. 1940) who became his frontline partner in his regular band.

In fact, although Coleman made the big splash, others had already been working on parallel lines. The pianist Cecil Taylor (b. 1930) had long been evolving a keyboard approach based on furious attack and dense textures, and continued to develop along his own lines through the Sixties, Seventies and Eighties. His music is more inaccessible and arguably more musically rich than Ornette Coleman's.

Another isolated experimenter was Sun Ra (1914–93), a musician who has the unique distinction among big band leaders of having been born on the planet Saturn (an alternative theory holds that he was once called Herman Blount, and came from Alabama.) Sun Ra started leading bands he called the Solar Orchestra in the Fifties (always with the tenor player John Gilmore), evolving towards a style which mixed musical freedoms with great theatricality. His musicians danced and processed, and might be dressed in spacesuits or flowing robes.

This theatricality was shared with the Art Ensemble of Chicago, a band containing the trumpeter Lester Bowie and reed players Joseph Jarman and Roscoe Mitchell. The excitement of seeing this band live, its supporters claim, is much greater than that captured on its records. Another player from Chicago is the composer and multi-instrumentalist Anthony Braxton, a performer whose work is occasionally beautifully persuasive, but often forbiddingly recondite (he is interested in the mathematical aspects of music).

The New Thing was a not a unified style like bop or swing, so much as a collection of coteries. Taylor's music, for example, is not really compatible with Coleman's. Also it is not so much a musical language as a Platonic ideal. Many musicians, for example the altoist Jackie McLean and multi-instrumentalist Eric Dolphy, moved more or less "outside", as it was called, the boundaries of bop.

How to sum it all up? As with much that happened in the Sixties, there were many experiments attempted that didn't work, and few solutions found. It was often most strikingly expressive when simplest —closest to the blues, the dirge, the cry. But to get to the bit that worked, the listener often had to sit through lengthy stretches of

Tenor saxophonist Archie Shepp was one of the most aggressive voices in the Sixties' New Thing.

rebarbative and self-indulgent chaos. Not surprisingly, it never developed much of an audience in the USA.

Free jazz found more of a home in northern Europe, where it fitted into the existing tradition of esoteric modern classical music. Many of the most prominent European players of the Sixties were affected by the free-jazz movement, including German trombonist Albert Mangelsdorff and British baritone saxophonist John Surman. It was in fact in the free jazz movement of the Sixties that European jazz at last began to attain autonomy from America.

FUSION

Jazz in the seventies

B Y THE LATE SIXTIES JAZZ WAS RAPIDLY LOSING ITS AUDIENCE. BEBOP AND SWING WERE BOTH OLD HAT, THOUGH EACH HAD HAD THEIR ADHERENTS, AND FREE JAZZ, THE NEW MOVEMENT OF THE EARLY SIXTIES, HAD NEVER WON MUCH OF AN AUDIENCE OUTSIDE EUROPE.

In New York it was to be found much more often in the low rent lofts of Manhattan than in commercial clubs. But even big stars like Miles Davis were finding their record sales and concert attendances dipping. Not for the first, or last, time people started to talk about the death of jazz. Something had to be done, and once again, it was Miles Davis who did it.

Miles's conclusion was that jazz had got dangerously out of touch with its natural constituency—young, urban Afro-Americans. After bop, they had slowly drifted away. Bop and cool were not very danceable. The New Thing was even less—all the person on the street could hear were a lot of very unappealing squeaks and gibbers. The popular black music had long been soul or electric blues. The jazz audience had in fact become largely middle class and white; even the younger middle-class white listeners had now turned more or less exclusively to rock.

Miles decided that if you can't beat them, you might as well join them. He started to listen hard to Sly And The Family Stone, a pop-soul-rock band that was very successful in 1968. And, slowly at first, he began to move in

the same direction. On *Miles In The Sky*, *Filles De Kilimanjaro* (both 1968) and *In A Silent Way* there are new sidesmen—the keyboard players Chick Corea and Joe Zawinul, British bassist Dave Holland and guitarist John McLaughlin—and the sound was becoming electric. But the breakthrough album was *Bitches Brew* (1969), which added a new drummer—Jack DeJohnette—and unveiled a completely new style: jazz-rock fusion.

Bitches Brew is one of the most divisive jazz albums ever made. To some it is another of Miles's great steps forward, a session to put beside *Birth Of The Cool* and *Kind Of Blue*. To others it marked the point where he ceased to be of serious musical interest—and these were not necessarily the nostagic, ageing fans of his earlier work; they also include the young neo-classical beboppers of the Eighties like Wynton Marsalis.

But Davis never looked back. He adopted an electric trumpet with a wa-wa device and performed in ever more thunderously amplified contexts until retiring from music in

1976 for a period of intense dissipation and near mental breakdown. After he returned in 1981, he continued to toy with pop and disco sounds.

His sidemen of the Sixties were quick to follow suit.

Within a year or two all of them had launched their own fusion bands: Chick Corea formed Return To Forever (a gloriously period name, that); Zawinul and Shorter, Weather Report; John McLaughlin, the Mahavishnu Orchestra; Jack DeJohnette, Special Edition. All were very successful. Soon more or less everybody was doing it, and hard bop trumpeters whose ambitions had previously barely extended to a sports car were flying around in private planes. These were delirious times; the most lucrative days for jazz musicians since the heyday of swing.

Nor was jazz-rock the only variety of fusion going on; soon just about any musical form you can mention was being fused with jazz, and anything else that came to mind. John McLaughlin went in for Indian music and flamenco; Chick Corea added Latin flavouring while the Brazilian

Miles Davis as pop star. Only his face, he said, had escaped the effects of his hard living.

Miles Davis's keyboards man Chick Corea went on to fuse various musical genres.

percussionist Airto worked with Miles Davis and Weather Report among others. His wife, the singer Flora Purim, joined him in Return To Forever. Latin jazz—which had been an accepted hybrid since Dizzy Gillespie started experimenting with it in the Forties—grew in popularity, and continued to do so dramatically through the Eighties. Keith Jarrett blended jazz with classical music and country and western—among other ingredients—in his epic, and very popular, solo piano improvisations.

This wasn't the end of the blending that went on. The notion of mixing jazz with native elements introduced the possiblity of jazz, or jazz-derived, music that didn't imitate the American original. The South African pianist Abdullah Ibrahim had been introducing African elements into jazz since the Sixties, and in the Seventies and Eighties his music took on a more and more indigenous colouring. Others followed the same path.

In Europe the Norwegian Jan Garbarek, after working with various permutations of freedom and fusion, began to explore the folk music of Scandinavia and developed a bleak northern idiom which has little to do with Armstrong or Basie but has found a large audience. This Euro-sound has appealed to other players like John Surman and saxophonist Tommy Smith in Britain.

How much of this was good music is another question. The first wave of jazz rock was often very slight stuff, if fun—Corea's Return To Forever is a perfect example. As the vogue wore on, the fusion bands

got lighter and lighter weight. Much of their music lacks the virtues of both jazz and rock. As for the other blends on the market—Garbarek and Jarrett, for example—they too have very few of the traditional qualities of jazz, but they have nevertheless found an audience. Up to a point the question, "Is it jazz?" is academic—the term "improvised music" is often preferred for the more remote varieties of freedom and fusion. But the blurring of jazz identity in the Seventies undoubtedly led to its reassertion by the young neo-classicists of the Eighties.

The urge to fuse is by no means dead, however. Rock inflections and techniques colour the work of John Scofield and Bill Frisell (b. 1951), for example, two guitarists who have been very prominent in recent years. And in search of a truly contemporary idiom the altoist Steve Coleman and band M-Base have attempted to fuse post-free jazz with hip-hop. As with so much fusion, the final product is not as good as the ingredients which went into it.

NEO-CLASSICISM

Exploring Jazz History

IN THE EIGHTIES JAZZ ENTERED ITS POST MODERNIST PHASE.
AS FAR AS STYLISTIC DEVELOPMENT WAS CONCERNED, IT SEEMED TO
HAVE RUN THE WHOLE GAMUT FROM—AS IT WERE—PLAINSONG
TO STOCKHAUSEN IN ABOUT 70 YEARS. NO FURTHER DEVELOPMENT
WAS CONCEIVABLE ALONG THOSE LINES.

After the Seventies, jazz had been fused with every imaginable kindred and unkindred form. Not a great deal more could be done along those lines either. Jazz today has no dominating figure—no Parker, no Coltrane, no Ornette Coleman. Instead we have a number of independent coteries. With the exception of those who continue to aim for some kind of fusion—including Steve Coleman and M-Base, Bill Frisell and John Scofield—most jazz in the Eighties and Nineties has been involved in one way or another with the exploration of jazz history.

Among the first to turn to jazz history were the young white musicians whose inspiration comes essentially from swing, with an added element of bop. The key figures here were the tenor saxophonist Scott Hamilton (b. 1954) and the cornettist Warren Vache (b. 1951), both of whom appeared on the New York scene in the late Seventies and were immediately acclaimed by both fans and players alike. In their wake have followed a steady stream of recruits to this kind of jazz.

In the Eighties the virtuoso guitarist Howard Alden appeared from California, and with him Dan Barrett, a trombonist who plays with great accomplishment in the manner of Jack Teagarden, Dicky Wells and the other great men of the Thirties. Around the same time Ken Peplowski began to make excellent records on which he played several reed instruments, but increasingly, and most impressively, the clarinet. The newest of these jazz young fogeys is Harry Allen, another outstanding tenor-player, still only in his mid twenties.

But—with the occasional exception—this approach has not much appealed to black musicians. They too, however, have been interested in history. Here the most prominent figures have been the Marsalis brothers, Wynton (b. 1961) and Branford (b. 1960) from New Orleans. Wynton—a trumpet player of extraordinary virtuosity—is especially passionate about maintaining the purity of the jazz tradition. His evolution, however, has been more complex. Starting in the late bop tradition of Art Blakey's Jazz Messengers, he was for a while audibly fascinated by Miles Davis's work of the mid Sixties, then began an exploration of earlier jazz history — Armstrong, Ellington, Morton — without as yet evolving a completely convincing synthesis of all these influences. In this delving into history Wynton has been followed by his pianist, Marcus Roberts, who performed Ellington and Jelly Roll pieces on a recent record.

Branford Marsalis, on the other hand, has stuck to a super-sophisticated amalgam of late Fifties/early Sixties tenor saxophone playing—especially Coltrane and Rollins—which has in turn had an influence on musicians like the British tenor player Courtney Pine. It is probably the lead of Wynton, however, which was decisive in encouraging an even younger group of black American musicians to take up bebop—among them the splendid and fiery trumpeter Roy Hargrove, altoist Antonio Hart, the pianist Mulgrew Miller, plus a number of tenor saxophonists, of whom the most notable is

perhaps Joshua Redman. The white altoist Christopher Hollyday—a Jackie McLean follower—belongs with this group too.

Wynton Marsalis got the publicity, but perhaps a more successful eclectic traditionalist has been the altoist Bobby Watson. Another graduate of the Messengers—though of a slightly earlier edition—Watson probably has the widest stylistic reach of anyone in jazz. Basically, he plays bop. But he can also perform convincingly in the style of Johnny Hodges, and for a while

worked with the swing big band the Savoy Sultans. With the 29th Street Saxophone Quartet—one of many unaccompanied all-saxophone groups which emerged in the Seventies and Eighties—he would move from passages suggesting a big band reed section to free jazz.

Also trying to perform the whole of jazz history at the same time—but from a different perspective—has been the group around the tenor player David Murray. Murray's point of departure was free jazz, from which his recorded work constitutes a long journey back towards the jazz tradition. His playing still has free elements, but, to judge from recordings, less and less. A number of sometime free jazz figures have taken the same path as Murray—Archie Shepp, for example. And with him should be grouped three brilliant and eclectic trombonists all born in the Fifties: Craig Harris, who has played in Murray's bands, George Lewis and Ray Anderson.

Tenor saxophonist Branford Marsalis is the eldest of the three jazz-playing sons of pianist Ellis Marsalis.

VOCAL JAZZ

Blues, Ballads
and Scat

T HE SINGING OF JAZZ IS A TRICKY BUSINESS. ESSENTIALLY, JAZZ IS A MATTER OF ALTERING A GIVEN THEME—EMBELLISHING IT, IMPROVISING, GIVING IT A DIFFERENT PHRASING. IN THE CASE OF INSTRUMENTAL MUSIC, OF COURSE, THIS IS EASY ENOUGH.

But the singer has an extra problem: the words. A song consists of music and lyrics, bonded together into a unit—if you tinker about with that too much the whole thing may become unglued. There are, of course, ways round this difficulty. But the special problems of jazz singing have given it a slightly separate history from the rest of the music.

Whether such performers as Bessie Smith, Ma Rainey and Clara Smith belong strictly speaking to the history of jazz is a matter of arbitrary classification. But they recorded most of their finest work with jazz musicians—often great ones—and the soaring strength of their music was close in spirit to early jazz. Strangely, though the classic blues singers were all female—and mostly, though not related, called Smith—their immediate successors were male.

As well as rivalling her physical bulk, Little Jimmy Rushing (1902–72) and Big Joe Turner (1911–85) had obvious musical affinities with Bessie Smith. But they belonged to the generation of south-western jazz that included players like Lester Young and Count Basie. Bessie's blues were slow and stately; Rushing and Turner were happy bustling along at the pace of a swing

band. Rushing worked exclusively in the jazz ambit, for many years with the Basie band. Turner—a performer with a stirringly mighty voice—was an integral part of the Kansas City jazz scene in the Thirties, performing with the boogie-woogie pianist Pete Johnson. He also had a period as a rock and roll star.

But in some ways the history of jazz singing really starts with Louis

Bessie Smith: big, strong, liquor-loving and as formidable in person as she sounds on record.

Armstrong. At first hearing, the grunts, "Oh Yeah's", "boz doz vats" and indescribable throaty prolongations of words may sound embarrassingly folksy. If you listen closely, you discover each sigh and casual-sounding bar of scat is musically perfect. Indeed, it was partly by these means that he was able to apply the same arts of subtle recomposition—shifting a note here, adding an emphasis there—to his vocal performances that he used when playing a melody on the trumpet.

From Louis descend most of the popular singers of the century, and almost all those in jazz. Following his example, a vast number of jazz instrumentalists would essay the occasional vocal chorus. Some, like Fats Waller, with his devastating way of lampooning the lyric he

was singing, were very good. The trombonist Jack Teagarden had an eerily floating sense of time, a world weary air, and a raffish slur

to his phrasing—all of which make his 'St James Infirmary', for example, a great, highly personal blues peformance. Others, such as Roy Eldridge and Dizzy Gillespie, only intended their vocals as light relief, but even if they had little in the way of voice, those men had a knowledge of phrasing that many professional singers lack.

32

Among Armstrong's singing disciples, the most important was Billie Holiday. The essence of her art—sweetness and relaxation, and she recorded with much the same sort of star-laden swing group as Billie Holiday. Wiley was the most delectably stylish of jazz singers. She confined herself to giving the melody a lovely satiny gloss, and each perfectly placed word a delicate emotional spin—wry, amused, tender—and always sounds very grown up, as if she'd been through it all, and come out with composure unruffled.

The way she would drag a phrase back against the beat, ease out a melodic line, after a chord—all this is directly or indirectly descended from Armstrong. Her personal addition was a throat-catching emotional poignancy which was beyond his cheery range. But there were other singers of her generation who came close at times to rivalling her quality. Among these were several singers who shared her great rhythmic ease, but lacked that emotional intensity.

The young Ella Fitzgerald was one. Maxine Sullivan (1911–87) was another—a marvellously deft performer who had a remarkable late flowering. A big name in the Thirties, she came out of retirement in the last two decades of her life sounding even better than before.

Two white singers—Lee Wiley (1915–75) and Mildred Bailey

(1907–51)—were in the same exalted class. Bailey's work had a special maddening, but it enjoyed a vogue in the Fifties, as performed by King Pleasure and the trio Lambert, Hendricks and Ross.

One of Armstrong's key innovations was scat—the art of singing invented nonsense syllables to an improvised line. Most good jazz singers scat—Ella Fitzgerald and Sarah Vaughan are or were past masters of it. One or two performers, like Leo Watson in the Thirties and the bop singer Babs Gonzales (1919–80), have specialized in it, and it plays an important in the work of Betty Carter, the most important singer to emerge after Vaughan. An odd derivative of scat was the practice of vocalese, whereby new lyrics are fitted to a recorded jazz solo by

To a large extent, the history of jazz singing since the Second World War is the story of Fitzgerald, O'Day, Vaughan, Carmen McRae and Carter (discussed elsewhere). Alone of those, however, O'Day gave rise to a school of her own. It was undoubtedly her approach which inspired the girl singers associated with cool jazz. June Christy (1926–90) was the singer with the Stan Kenton band in the late Forties. Chris Connor (b. 1929) also worked with Kenton and continues in excellent voice today. Both are singers who, in their smooth, mellow, rather detached manner can be extremely good.

But Betty Carter's influence can perhaps be detected in Cassandra Wilson, a singer who mixes rock and rap with her jazz, and was the most interesting new vocalist to appear in the Eighties.

some instrumentalist. It is hard to decide whether this is marvellous or

CANNONBALL ADDERLEY

The alto saxophonist Julian "Cannonball" Adderley (the nickname was a corruption of "cannibal" and refers to his remarkable appetite for food) was one of the major popularizers of jazz in the late Fifties and Sixties. Essentially, he did for the alto what Horace Silver did in his piano playing and compositions—take the bebop idioms back to their roots in gospel and blues. The stirringly churchy sound of Cannonball's saxophone made him sound distinct—as most Fifties altoists did not—from Charlie Parker. The fame of the band he co-led with his cornettist brother Nat also rested on the soul-rich, sanctified gospel idiom.

Born in 1928, Adderley organized high school bands in his native Florida until his dramatic descent on New York in 1955, when he sat in at the Café Bohemia and was immediately recognized as a new star. He worked with his brother and Miles Davis—he is on the classic *Kind Of Blue* (1959)—then formed the quintet which became one of the most popular bands of the Sixties. 'Mercy, Mercy, Mercy!' was Number 11 in the US singles charts in 1966. Musically, the most successful moments on record came early, on the Riverside albums. But Cannonball remained a big name until his sudden death from a stroke in 1975.

HOWARD ALDEN

Born in 1958, Howard Alden was just 4 when the Beatles made their first LP, yet he found his way back to the music of Charlie Christian, Django Reinhardt, Barney Kessel and Joe Pass, all of whom are audible influences on the formation of his style. Like those men, Alden has an ability to produce a lucid progression of inter-related, neatly resolved ideas. His sound is mellow, rounded and entirely without the rabble-rousing oratory of rock, funk or fusion. He is certainly one of the

who's who

most versatile and impressive new musicians to emerge in the Eighties.

Alden—who hails from California—has been ubiquitous recently in the mainstream jazz circles of New York. Firstly, he is co-leader with the trombonist Dan Barrett of the Alden-Barrett Quintet, a spritely and unhackneyed little band for which the veteran trumpeter Buck Clayton wrote a number of beautiful scores. But Alden has also been the favoured musical partner of both the cornettist Ruby Braff and the clarinettist Kenny Davern. Further, in the last couple of years he has formed a performing and recording duo with one of his greatest heroes, the veteran guitarist George Van Eps (b. 1913), and done a good deal of recording on his own account, including a delightful album of acoustic guitar.

HENRY "RED" ALLEN

Born in 1908, the trumpeter Henry "Red" Allen was the last great musician to come out of the New Orleans school. Louis Armstrong had already left town by the time that Allen was forming his style, but it was as a rival to Satchmo that Allen was first seen by record companies. The recordings he made in New York in 1929 used the same formula as Armstrong's early big band performances. But in retrospect the differences between the two are more conspicuous than the resemblances. Armstrong's playing—calm and measured—resembled great oratory. Allen's playing was wilder, freer and more

Guitarist Howard Alden—as happy playing James P. Johnson as Thelonious Monk—is one of the most talented guitarists to have emerged in recent times.

loosely constructed, more like excitable conversation. He made a number of marvellous recordings in 1929–30 under his own name, 'Biff'ly Blues' and 'Feelin' Drowsy' among them. He is also prominent on records with the Luis Russell band, and later in the Thirties with such colleagues as the tenor saxophonist Coleman Hawkins and the trombonist J. C. Higginbotham.

Unlike some of his contemporaries, Allen continued to develop for several decades and, by the Fifties, he had

Trumpeter Henry "Red" Allen's traditional jazz was wild and free enough to attract the ear of the Sixties' avant-garde.

evolved one of the most richly eccentric styles in jazz, constructing long wandering lines which moved sighs and murmurs to suddenly hoarse shouts, and unexpected leaps from low to high register. This kind of playing led the experimental trumpeter Don Ellis to describe Allen—then in his sixties—as the most avant-garde trumpeter in New York. He died in 1967.

LOUIS ARMSTRONG

See separate entry in the Legends section.

CHET BAKER

Chet Baker was a trumpet player with the soft-textured, wistful sound similar to that of Miles Davis, but without Davis's smouldering emotional undercurrents.

Baker was born in 1929 and shot to prominence with the Gerry Mulligan Quartet of 1952. His early work had a fresh lyricism reminiscent of Bix Beiderbecke but, like Beiderbecke, he went rapidly into decline, heroin being just one of his vices. For a while his James Dean looks and romantic playing made him one of the icons of Fifties jazz. But in the Sixties things began to go sour. In 1968 he lost his teeth in a drugs-related fight. This is normally a catastrophe for a brass player, but somehow Baker managed to resume playing. His late work has its moving moments, but it is notable more for the sad autobiography it reflects than for any musical brilliance.

By the end the James Dean look-alike had developed a visage astonishingly seamed and fissured with lines and wrinkles. *Let's Get Lost*, the film made about Baker shortly before his death in 1988 in an unexplained fall from an Amsterdam hotel window, is a document both melancholy and sinister.

COUNT BASIE

Born in 1904, William "Count" Basie was a north-eastern stride pianist—at one point he took informal organ lessons from his contemporary, Fats Waller—who landed up in Kansas City. There he became pianist in the finest south-western band, Bennie Moten's. Then, after Moten's death, he became a bandleader himself. He returned to New York at the head of one of the greatest ensembles jazz has ever seen, stuffed with superb musicians from the South-West. By this stage he himself was playing a sort of minimalist stride, so pared down that he might play a half a dozen notes in twice as many bars. Basie was an outstanding exponent of the dictum "less is more".

His wonderful early band was to some extent a group achievement, with soloists like Lester Young and Buck Clayton contributing ideas for collective "head" arrangements. But Basie was a great leader, and he showed his mettle when the big-band business crashed in the late Forties, and he was forced to disband. He formed first an octet, then within a couple of years a brand new band, full of new faces which swept the country. The Basie bands of the Fifties, Sixties and Seventies were more arranged and regimented affairs than the pre-war model—machines for swinging—but they always sounded good. Basie, a superb talent scout, came up with a new generation of wonderful soloists, among them the trumpeter Joe Newman, saxophonists Frank Foster and Lockjaw Davis, and trombonist Al Grey. He died in 1984.

SIDNEY BECHET

Soaring, passionate, endlessly inventive, mesmerizingly eloquent, the clarinettist and soprano saxophonist Sidney Bechet would figure on most shortlists of the greatest soloists in jazz. He was a natural talent who started very young, sitting in with the Freddie Keppard band, by his own account, at the age of 6. At the age of 17 he was off and on the road.

As early as 1919 he was in London, playing with the Will Marion Cook Band. It was then that he discovered the soprano which became his main instrument. Later he was deported as an undesirable alien after a fight with a prostitute in an hotel bedroom. Bechet recorded little in the Twenties, despite playing with some important bands, including Ellington's. In 1929 he became involved in a gunfight with another musician in a Paris street, wounding a passer-by and receiving a prison sentence.

But he was out of prison in time to make some superb recordings in 1932 with the New Orleans Feetwarmers (which he co-led with the trumpeter Tommy Ladnier). Like other New Orleans musicians, he was in the doldrums for much of the Thirties, at one point opening a tailoring shop. The bulk of his finest recordings were made in New York in the Forties for the RCA and Blue Note companies. There were also a very fine series of duets with the white clarinettist Mezz Mezzrow on King Jazz. Bechet moved to France in 1951, where, somewhat mellowed, he became a national figure and died in 1959.

Cornetist Bix Beiderbecke played with extraordinary brilliance and originality for a few years in the Twenties, then drank himself to death.

BIX BEIDERBECKE

Born in 1903, the young Bix was intended by his middle-class parents to follow a respectable career. But he discovered jazz early on—it was performed on the Mississippi river boats which stopped at his home town of Davenport—and never wanted to do anything afterwards but play it. He played around Chicago, then moved to New York where he worked for the famous Paul Whiteman Orchestra. At 25 he was a sensation among the new underground of jazz fans; at 28, in 1931, he was burnt out and dead of alcohol-induced pneumonia.

Until his first alcoholic breakdown at the beginning of 1929, Beiderbecke himself always performed superbly. But most of the many recordings he made in his short career were marred by the inferior company in which he played. By far the the most impressive of his records are the small group of tracks he made with the saxophonist Frankie Trumbauer in 1927. Of these, two—'Singing The Blues' and 'I'm Coming Virginia'—are jazz masterpieces by any standards, made, respectively, a month before and a month after Bix's twenty-fourth birthday.

Beiderbecke developed a ravishing style which is almost wholly original. His tone on the cornet was pure, open and one of the most sheerly beautiful sounds in jazz. Like Louis Armstrong, he improvised solos of interrelated phrases that added up to a whole—in effect, new compositions related to the theme. But the emotional substance of his music was quite different. Beiderbecke's most important achievement was the introduction of a new mood into jazz: intimate, poetic and lyrical.

BUNNY BERIGAN

The white trumpeter Bunny Berigan produced in 'I Can't Get Started' (1937) a flawless exercise in Armstrong's grand 'West End Blues' manner, laced with a touch of Beiderbecke's lyricism. It is one of the great jazz solos of the Thirties. Louis Armstrong liked it so much that apparently he preferred not to play that tune, he felt it belonged to Bunny. Armstrong is also said to have remarked that the only thing wrong with Berigan as a trumpeter was that he didn't live long enough.

Sadly, that was absolutely correct. Like many of his contemporaries, Berigan was an alcoholic, and the booze killed him in 1942 when he was in his mid thirties (he had been born in 1908). 'I Can't Get Started' was his finest hour. But he managed to record a good deal of excellent trumpet besides. He was a star of the early Benny Goodman band, worked a good deal with Tommy Dorsey, and led a big band of his own. Unfortunately, in company with many of the best improvisers of the day, he wasn't a very good business man or organizer, and his bands generally weren't worthy of him.

Like far too many brilliant jazz musicians of the period, he flared brilliantly for a short while before guttering out while he still had plenty to give.

ART BLAKEY

Art Blakey, born in 1919, was a member of the first bebop generation, and was fairly prominent in the Forties. But his real contribution belongs to another decade and to the world of late Fifties hard bop. As a drummer, Blakey had a stunning strength. He was fond of unleashing a press roll like an approaching avalanche, and of using his elbow to get a rapid series of different tones from a drum. The music was carried along on the great rolling wave of Blakey's drumming.

His importance, however, is as much as a leader as an instrumentalist. Blakey first recorded with a group called the Jazz Messengers (under Horace Silver's leadership) in 1954, and continued to lead groups with that name almost uninterruptedly for the rest of his life. Throughout this period, the Messengers functioned as a sort of graduate institute for fledgling players, or jazz cadet academy, instilling qualities of confidence and self-reliance in stars to be. Over the years, a huge number of important performers was nurtured by the Blakey band—among many others, the trumpeters Lee Morgan, Freddie Hubbard and Wynton Marsalis; the saxophonists Jackie McLean, Benny Golson, Wayne Shorter, Hank Mobley, Bobby Watson and Branford Marsalis.

It is probably more due to Blakey than to anyone else that bop remained a vital and popular idiom with young players in the late Eighties and early Nineties, 50 years after it had first been evolved. He died in 1991.

RUBY BRAFF

Cornetist Ruby Braff plays with a beautiful tone and melodic inventiveness.

The trumpeter and cornetist Ruby Braff is living proof that jazz need not move on a one-way historical path. Born in 1927, he is a contemporary of the cool and hard bop players of the Fifties, yet he is indubitably a major performer in the manner of men like Louis Armstrong and Bobby Hackett—an idiom whose day had allegedly passed before he made his first recording.

Braff came to prominence in a series of albums for the Bethlehem and Vanguard labels in 1954–55—which played a significant part in the Fifties rediscovery of swing or, as it was then called, "mainstream" jazz. By the Seventies and Eighties he had become a father-figure to a new generation of young mainstreamers, like the tenor player Scott Hamilton.

Braff is one of the most consistently inventive melodic improvisers in jazz, and one who flourishes in a chamber jazz context, whether duetting with the pianists Ellis Larkins and Dick Hyman, partnered by the guitarist George Barnes in a lithe quartet in the Seventies, or playing in the more recent trio featuring another guitarist, the youthful Howard Alden.

CLIFFORD BROWN

Clifford Brown was in many ways the supreme trumpeter in post-war jazz. Ten years younger than Charlie Parker (he was born in 1930), he came along at a time when the feverish, experimental days of bebop had passed. And, for the fire and dash of men like Parker and Gillespie, he substituted a noble, easy quality that at times puts one in mind of eighteenth-century classical music. Everything about his playing—the golden tone, the unbelievably fleet runs, the long, springing lines—had a mellow perfection. Which is probably why Brown—even more than Gillespie, or Miles Davis—has been the touchstone of excellence for the trumpeters of the last four decades. Even today there are few of them who do not have a little Brown in their soul.

This huge influence is all the more surprising because it was achieved in a very short period of time. Brown came to prominence in 1953, playing with Tadd Dameron and the Lionel Hampton band. Within a short space of time he had established himself as the brightest young star in the music. The Quintet which he co-led with the drummer Max Roach was the leading band of the day. Brown himself recorded with extraordinary profuseness, but without leaving an ugly chorus to posterity. Then, very quickly, it was over. He died in a car crash in June, 1956, several months short of his twenty-sixth birthday. It was one of the most grievous losses jazz has ever suffered.

DAVE BRUBECK

Dave Brubeck's stature as a jazz musician has been much derided over the years—perhaps unfairly. He and his Quartet were immensely popular with white college audiences in the Fifties. His album *Jazz Goes To College* made the Top 10 charts in 1954, Brubeck and his band consistently won music polls in the mid to late Fifties, and sold records in abundance—and this very success attracted critical fire. Brubeck himself was often seen as a stiff pianist, over-fond of classical devices—he had studied with Schoenberg and Darius Milhaud at one stage—and tricky time signatures (typified by his big hit, 'Take Five', from an album of time signature experiments, *Time Out*, 1959).

In fact, although Brubeck does not qualify as a major pianist, his bands were actually among the more enterprising and engaging of the cool school. And his partnership with the brilliant altoist Paul Desmond—continuous until 1967, then intermittent until Desmond's death in 1977—was one of the most long-lasting and productive in post war jazz. Desmond was an altoist to compare with Lee Konitz and Art Pepper, and almost all his best music was made with Brubeck. The pianist's work in latter years, however, has not been of great interest. Brubeck was born in 1920.

Benny Carter was among the very first to develop a jazz style on the alto saxophone. 60 years on, he remains among the best.

BENNY CARTER

Carter is one of the most versatile men in jazz, and, born way back in 1907, one of its great survivors. First and foremost, he ranks with Hodges and Parker among the music's finest alto saxophonists. His style is characterized by a high-stepping elegance of line, and an apparent ability to conceive an entire solo as an entity. He developed this approach in the late Twenties, and it has remained, except for a slight bop influence from the Forties on, unchanged to this day. But—a multi-instrumentalist—Carter has also recorded impressively on tenor, clarinet and trumpet. Also, he rates with Ellington and Henderson as an arranger of the swing period.

During the Thirties and early Forties Carter led a number of excellent, though not very successful, big bands for which he wrote with suavity and panache, especially for the reeds. In the mid to late Thirties, he spent a period in Europe, working for the BBC in London and recording with Coleman Hawkins and Django Reinhardt in Paris. In the Forties, he settled in California and started to work extensively as an arranger for films and television. Consequently, his jazz recordings in the Fifties and Sixties were more sporadic, though invariably impeccable. He remains today as urbane and musically active as ever, and recently celebrated his eighty-fifth birthday by releasing a double CD containing two brand new suites for big band and strings.

BETTY CARTER

No one has taken the human voice closer to the flexibility and adventurousness of instrumental jazz than Betty Carter. Her wordless improvisations on a theme—scat singing—may last as long as a marathon saxophone solo. Her vocal range and harmonic sophistication are extraordinary. In both respects her art is an extension of that of Sarah Vaughan. But the mood is very different. Vaughan's music was sybaritically lush; Carter's is often wry and sardonic. At her best, however, as on her astonishing medley of 'Body And Soul' and 'Heart And Soul', she shows a uniqueness of voice, an ability to squeeze meaning from a lyric, and to stretch and alter a melody without destroying its basic shape, which it it is not absurd to compare with Billie Holiday.

Her career has not progressed easily. Born in 1930, from 1948 to 1951 she worked with Lionel Hampton—who christened her "Betty Bebop". But her first significant recordings did not come until the 1958–61 period. And the albums did not amount to more than a trickle until she formed her own company—Bet-Car Records—which issued a number of live performances from the Seventies and Eighties. In recent years, however, she has been widely recognized as one of the most remarkable singers in jazz.

DOC CHEATHAM

Adolphus "Doc" Cheatham has had one of the longest, and also one of the oddest, careers in jazz. Born in 1905, he was accompanying Bessie Smith in his native Nashville in the early Twenties, and understudied Louis Armstrong in Chicago in 1926. He was a member of several respected big and small bands in the Thirties and Forties, notably Cab Calloway's. But he made very few recordings, and remained little known to the jazz public until the mid Seventies, when he had reached an age when many musicians have already retired.

His style is essentially based on Louis Armstrong's, with great purity of melodic invention, and stamina truly amazing in a player of his advanced years. Most of his best recordings date from the the last two decades, by which stage he had become almost the only surviving trumpeter from the Twenties—certainly the only one playing with such élan. As such, he has appeared in concerts with Wynton Marsalis, over half a century his junior, and appeared regularly throughout the world. In 1991 a huge array of trumpeters paid tribute to him at the New York Jazz Festival. He has announced that he would like to carry on playing until he is at least 90.

CHARLIE CHRISTIAN

Charlie Christian was the first player to develop a convincing style on the electrically amplified guitar. Christian discovered that amplification could give it the gravity and force of a tenor saxophone or trumpet, and it is from his music that almost all the jazz guitarists of the next two decades took their cue.

Christian, born in 1916, came from Oklahoma, and, in many ways, his was a typically South-Western style—uncluttered, loping, blues-based. He fitted beautifully into the swing sound of the Benny Goodman Sextet, although, harmonically, he was inclined to explore intervals then unusual. Most of his recordings were made with the Goodman Sextet between 1939 and 1941, and he also recorded an admirable concerto, 'Solo Flight', with the full Goodman band.

Christian also liked to jam in Harlem nightclubs with the leaders-to-be of the bop revolution—Dizzy Gillespie, Charlie Parker, Thelonious Monk, the drummer Kenny Clarke. A few recordings were made of these sessions, on which Christian stretches out for chorus after chorus in a way he was not able to do on commercial recordings. They give a glimpse of what might have been, had he not died so young of tuberculosis in 1942.

BUCK CLAYTON

Born in 1911, Clayton led a number of bands of his own, including one in Shanghai, before joining Count Basie in 1936. His early recordings in the following few years reveal him as an exceptionally delicate and lyrical follower of Louis Armstrong. Often he used mutes, and was at his very best in small group sessions with such fellow spirits as Lester Young and Billie Holiday.

After the war, however, he re-emerged, unlike some of his contemporaries, sounding better and more confident than ever. Clayton was a leading spirit in the renaissance of swing jazz under the new label, "mainstream", which occurred in the mid Fifties. At that time he made innumerable recordings, including the series of *Jam Sessions* for which he became best known. These, despite their informal-sounding title, also gave Clayton an opportunity to shine as an arranger.

In the late Sixties, he ran into a succession of health problems which eventually forced him to stop playing altogether. Undaunted, however, he returned to prominence in his seventies as an arranger and composer, and, by now a jazz patriarch, organized an admirable big band in New York in the late Eighties. He died in 1992.

One of the stars of the early Basie band, the trumpeter Buck Clayton went on to become a prominent figure in the mainstream jazz scene of the Fifties.

EDDIE CONDON

NAT "KING" COLE

Cole was a strange case of a performer whose vast success in one capacity almost obliterated his even greater abilities in another direction. He was, in the first place, not a singer at all, but one of the major jazz pianists of his era—the very end of the swing period, just merging into bop. Born in 1917, Cole was one of the most important disciples of Earl Hines, with a distinctively light, skipping approach to the keyboard; and the lithe drumless trio (piano, bass, guitar) which he formed in 1939 was one of the most successful groups of its day. By the Fifties and Sixties he had become a vocal superstar, and his piano-playing was consequently almost forgotten. Even so, he made a nostalgic return to jazz for one album—*After Hours*—recorded with various guest stars including the trumpeter Sweets Edison in 1956. He also recorded as a singer with the Stan Kenton and Count Basie bands (the latter minus Basie). Cole died in 1965.

ORNETTE COLEMAN

See separate entry in the *Legends* section.

JOHN COLTRANE

See separate entry in the *Legends* section.

Condon was a rhythm guitarist of some ability, but his real contribution to jazz was a different one—as an organizer and personality. Born in 1905 and hailing from the Midwest—Goodland, Indiana—he fell in with the circle of young white jazz musicians in Chicago, and was co-leader on one of their key early sessions, McKenzie and Condon's Chicagoans, 1927. He moved to New York in 1928 and recorded with, among others, Louis Armstrong and Fats Waller.

As the time wore on, Condon became the rallying point for this style of traditionalist jazz, and a spokesman for jazz in general. This was not so much because of his musical talents, as of his capacity to talk. Confident, articulate, a very heavy drinker and a noted wit, Condon slowly turned into a public figure. In the Forties, he organized a series of broadcast jam sessions at New York Town Hall, including a number of important black musicians as well as white traditionalists. Then, building on this success, he opened a club in New York which became a home for the sort of jazz he believed in.

In later years Condon's playing was not always audible on recordings; but he never failed to convey his own brash jaunty spirit to every group he led. In 1948 he published *We Called It Music*, one of the best jazz autobiographies. He died in 1973.

Renowned as bandleader, drinker and raconteur, Condon once gave his formula for a hangover cure: "Take the juice of one quart of Bourbon."

CHICK COREA

One of the most popular musicians to emerge from the jazz fusion movement, Chick Corea—like many another jazz star—was groomed for the limelight in the Miles Davis finishing school. Born in 1941, he had worked with Herbie Mann and the Latin percussionist Mongo Santamaria before joining Davis in 1968. But it was his work in Miles's revolutionary jazz-rock bands that really made his name. He appears with Miles on *In a Silent Way*, *Bitches Brew* (both 1969), *Live/Evil* (1970) and *On The Corner* (1972)—the ground-breaking jazz rock albums.

His subsequent career has been marked by an alternation between this jazz-rock idiom—exploited by his own Seventies band Return To Forever, and an effort to fuse jazz with Latin and classical elements. He remains extremely popular in both capacities, running in recent years both an Electric Band and an Akoustic Band, plus soloing in 1993 as an (acoustic) solo pianist. None the less, most of his Seventies and Eighties work is very slight, and some would say—this writer included—that even at his best he is rather short on solid jazz virtues.

BOB CROSBY

Bob, brother of Bing, was the only bandleader of the swing era to be hired by his own musicians. A forgettable singer, he was selected by the leaderless men of the ex-Ben Pollack band as a suitable person to stand in front of them. In effect, the band was a co-operative, and one of a very interesting kind: it was made up of young white players who disliked the regimentation of orthodox swing and hankered after the freedoms of the Twenties.

In the Thirties, every band had to have a leader. A group of dixielanders chose Bing Crosby's brother as theirs.

The Bob Crosby Band included at one time most of the best traditionalists who came along in the Thirties, including the trumpeters Yank Lawson and Billy Butterfield, the clarinettist Irving Fazola and the tenor player Eddie Miller. The bass player, Bob Haggart, came up with much of the material—one piece, a feature for Butterfield named 'I'm Free', was later rechristened as the standard 'What's New'. At its best the Crosby Band—for example in 'South Rampart Street Parade'—brought a great deal of the looseness of Chicago and New Orleans

to the big band ensemble, and even more, of course, to their small band, the Bob Cats.

The various bands led by Lawson and Haggart after the war—most notably the World's Greatest Jazz Band of the Seventies and Eighties—were continuations of the Crosby ethos. Born in 1913, Crosby lived until 1993.

TADD DAMERON

Born in 1917, Tadd Dameron was the first arranger to adapt the harmonic sophistications of bebop to a large ensemble. But the mood of his music was very far from the fire and fury of Gillespie or Bud Powell. Indeed, it was lucidly elegant in sound in a way that recalls the work of swing composers like Benny Carter. Dameron insisted that "when I write something, it's with beauty in mind", a beauty which came in part from harmonic luxuriance. Dexter Gordon called him "the romanticist of the whole period", and remembered that even when playing a third saxophone part by Dameron, shivers would run down his spine because the music was so lovely.

Dameron contributed some of the finest scores to the early Dizzy Gillespie big band. Then, in the late Forties, he organized a little group of his own which featured a fellow-spirit in Fats Navarro, a trumpeter who also emphasized melodic beauty within a bop context.

The two were unfortunately linked by another factor besides an interest in beauty—heroin addiction. As a result

Dameron only produced a few more albums, among them the marvellous *Fontainebleau* (1956). He spent much of his later life in prison and died in 1965.

KENNY DAVERN

Kenny Davern is without doubt the greatest traditional jazz clarinettist in the world today: a description which suggests that he must be a performer both of rare quality and of splendid indifference to passing trends. And indeed that is exactly what he is.

His music derives from the early clarinettists of New Orleans and Chicago—Jimmy Noone, Pee Wee Russell, Irving Fazola. But he avoids the trap of simple imitation. Davern is clearly his own man, and has a surprising width of musical sympathy; he once recorded with the avant-gardist Steve Lacy, and expressed admiration for Ornette Coleman. Despite—or because of—his conservatism, Davern has been one of the most committed and exciting improvisers of the Seventies and Eighties.

As a young man (he was born in 1935), Davern played with Jack Teagarden, and appeared on one of the last recordings Eddie Condon made. But he first came to real prominence in the mid Seventies with Soprano Summit, a quintet he co-led with Bob Wilber. Both played soprano saxophone (though also clarinet and alto), though subsequently Davern has concentrated on clarinet alone. Another fruitful musical partnership was with the superb

stride pianist, Dick Wellstood (1927–87), which resulted in some of the finest traditional/mainstream recordings of the last 20 years.

EDDIE "LOCKJAW" DAVIS

A tremendously tough and assertive tenor saxophonist, Lockjaw Davis fitted into no pigeon-hole. Born in 1922, he came to prominence in the Forties—when he got his nickname from taking part in a series of records named after diseases, one of which was lockjaw. His harmonic and rhythmic habits fitted in well enough with bop—he recorded with Fats Navarro—but his unforgettable, side-of-the-mouth tone belonged more to the world of late swing.

Like many musicians with a foot in both bop and pre-bop camps, Davis found a home in the post-war Basie band, where he stayed from 1952 to 1953. More memorably from the recording point of view, he also worked with the band on the classic *Atomic Mr Basie* of 1957. On this he took a celebrated up-tempo solo on 'Whirlibird', arguably his very finest. He was with Basie again from 1966 to 1973. In between he spent some time in a two-tenor band with Johnny Griffin, and more in groups of his own with organ—most memorably played by Shirley Scott—bass and drums. Towards the end of his life (he died in 1986) he formed another musical partnership with the trumpeter Harry "Sweets" Edison.

ERIC DOLPHY

Eric Dolphy, born in 1928, was one of the most questing musicians of his generation. A multi-instrumentalist, he was a forerunner of the tendency among Sixties avant-gardists to move from one musical voice to another. Dolphy played alto saxophone, flute and clarinet, but perhaps his most distinctive contributions were on bass clarinet, a rare instrument of which he was the virtual pioneer in jazz. Less messianic than Coltrane, less drastically radical than Ornette Coleman, none the less he was to the forefront of those who were attempting to find a way beyond bebop in the early Sixties.

He came to prominence quite late, as a member of the West Coast Chico Hamilton group from 1958 to 1960. Then for a while in New York he was everywhere on the jazz cutting edge—playing in some of Charles Mingus's wildest groups, working briefly with Coltrane, and appearing on a plethora of recordings, Ornette Coleman's celebrated Free Jazz among them. His very finest recorded moments, however, came on albums recorded in partnership with the short-lived trumpeter Booker Little —notably Far Cry (1961), and, even better, his own Out To Lunch (1964), one of the classic recordings of the era. He died suddenly of diabetes while on tour in Europe the same year.

Multi-instrumentalist Eric Dolphy was one of the most impressive musical explorers of the Sixties, and the first player to find a jazz voice for the bass clarinet.

MILES DAVIS

See separate entry in the Legends section.

JOHNNY DODDS

One of the greatest and most forceful of New Orleans clarinettists, Dodds recorded prolifically in Chicago in the Twenties. Born in 1892, he was a member of the classic King Oliver Creole Jazz Band (which Dodds and his brother, the drummer, Warren "Baby" Dodds left after they discovered Oliver was cheating them out of money). In this context he played in the fluid style associated with the creole musicians of New Orleans (Dodds himself was black). But later he developed a much more forceful, blues-based approach. No one, except for Sidney Bechet, blew the clarinet as hard.

Dodds can be heard playing in this vein on Louis Armstrong's superb series of Hot Five and Hot Seven recordings made in 1925–27, on which he sometimes seems to be trying to out-play the great trumpeter. He also recorded with Jelly Roll Morton (among other things, some splendid trio tracks with Morton on piano and Baby Dodds on drums), and with bands he led himself. Dodds continued to work regularly as musician through the Forties, but did not record again until shortly before his death in 1940 at the relatively early age of 48.

ROY ELDRIDGE

Born in 1911, Roy Eldridge was the greatest trumpeter to come along between Louis Armstrong in the Twenties and Dizzy Gillespie in the Forties. In contrast to Armstrong, Eldridge emphasized mobility; he played faster, and constructed looser, wilder sounding phrases. But at an early stage he was also struck by Armstrong's ability to "tell a story"—construct a solo that was an architectural unity—and he added a sense of structure to his passionate style.

His early prime was the late Thirties, when he recorded solos of extraordinary fire and brio with his own small groups and with the bands of Henderson, Gene Krupa and Artie Shaw. As his follower Dizzy Gillespie's star rose in the Forties, Eldridge started to sound unsettled, and some of his work from that period is brash. By the Fifties, however, he was back on form, playing now with a sizzling vibrato. During that period, he recorded much with Gillespie and recorded magnificent music with colleagues like Oscar Peterson, Lester Young and Coleman Hawkins. His technique was, however, too demanding to last comfortably into old age, and he gave up playing in the late Seventies. He died in 1988.

DUKE ELLINGTON

See separate entry in the Legends section.

GIL EVANS

One of the half-dozen great arrangers in jazz, Gil Evans had a slow musical start. A Canadian born in 1912, and an obscure bandleader in the Thirties, it was not until the late Forties that he became an important jazz innovator. At that stage, he became, in the words of fellow arranger George Russell, a "guru" whose New York apartment was a sort of club for the avant-garde of jazz. His first important arrangements were for the Claude Thornhill Band, whose moody, clouded sound was Evans's invention. He applied the same principles in his scores for the Miles Davis Nonet, whose immensely influential style was again based on Evans's ideas.

But little more was heard from Evans himself until 1957, when he again collaborated with Davis to produce a marvellous soloist-plus-big band album, *Miles Ahead*. There followed a string of projects with Davis, and Evans started to record in his own right. The albums of the late Fifties and early Sixties are his finest achievement. But, ever an innovator, he was attracted to the rock and jazz-rock fusion sound of the later Sixties and Seventies. Having formed highly praised fusion bands, he died in 1988.

ART FARMER

Reflective, melodic, beautiful, the sounds of Art Farmer's trumpet and flugelhorn have been ubiquitous in jazz since the Fifties.

Art Farmer is one of those musicians who make no notable innovation, yet none the less succeed in adding an individual contribution to jazz. His trumpet—and, latterly, flugelhorn—has the clouded, melodic quality of Miles Davis (whose parts he played in the 1992 revival of the

BILL EVANS

Bill Evans was the most significant pianist to appear since Bud Powell had emerged in the Forties—the first to offer a completely new approach to the keyboard. In a famous comparison, Lalo Shifrin likened Oscar Peterson to Liszt, Evans to Chopin. Certainly a reflective, delicate mood related to classical piano music was Evans's most distinctive contribution to jazz.

Born in 1929, he was at first a reluctant recording artist, making a début album in 1956, then nothing more until 1958, when he produced the magnificent *Everyone Digs Bill Evans* for Riverside, with Philly Joe Jones on drums. After this the records came with a rush. Evans was the pianist with the 1959 Miles Davis Sextet which introduced the concept of modal jazz to a wide jazz audience—and his contribution was second only to that of the leader himself.

Next he formed a trio with the innovatory and short-lived bassist Scott LaFaro which culminated in a live recording at the Village Vanguard which in the opinion of many is one of the supreme jazz recordings of the period. Ten days later LaFaro was killed in a car accident.

In the early to mid Sixties Evans made a stream of recordings, with his trio, solo, multi-tracked with himself, and with the guitarist Jim Hall. These were his great days. By the late Sixties he sounded a trifle stale, and, plagued as he was by heroin addiction, his career was increasingly erratic. He died in 1980.

late Forties Birth Of The Cool band). But Farmer is by no means a Davis clone; he is a musician, like the tenor players Zoot Sims and Stan Getz, who forms a sort of modern mainstream, occupying the wide centre-ground of post-war jazz. His music is marked by a tranquil lyricism which can sometimes make it seem undramatic; he has none of Miles Davis's underlying venom.

His career has been varied and busy, and marked by a number of musical partnerships. Born in 1928, after playing in the Lionel Hampton band beside Clifford Brown, he formed his own quintet in 1955 with the alto saxophonist Gigi Gryce as front-line partner. From 1959 to 1960 he co-led the Jazztet with tenor saxophonist Benny Golson (the band was reformed in the mid Eighties). Then from 1963 to 1964 he formed a quartet with the dulcet guitarist, Jim Hall.

Farmer settled in Vienna in 1968, and has lived there ever since, although he continues to tour widely and record regularly in the Eighties and Nineties.

ELLA FITZGERALD

An orphan from Yonkers, a suburb of New York, Ella Fitzgerald became a singer almost by accident. Born in 1918, she entered an amateur talent contest at the age of 15 as a dancer, and only began to sing because stage fright rendered her incapable of movement. From then on, however, her career has an air of inevitability. The following year, 1934, she joined the Chick Webb band, and soon became its major attraction. At this stage her voice had not attained the astonishing creamy richness of her maturity, but she already had an extraordinary rhythmic deftness, which made her one of the major swing-era singers. In 1938 she had a big hit with 'A-Tisket, A-Tasket', and when Webb died the following year, she took over as leader.

She continued to work and record busily through the Forties, but the Fifties were her great decade. By this stage her voice was at a peak of perfection, and she had acquired an easy mastery of the ballad. The attraction of her work, however, lies in the sheer beauty of the sound, plus a straight-down-the-middle directness of interpretation. She does not attempt the emotional drama of a Billie Holiday (and her private life has been comparatively uneventful).

In the Fifties she made remarkable recordings with Louis Armstrong, and the pianist Ellis Larkins, plus the monumental Songbook series of albums for Verve, devoted to the music of Cole Porter, Gershwin, Rodgers and Hart, Duke Ellington and others. These are her masterpieces. From the mid Sixties on, her vocal powers declined somewhat. She last recorded in 1989, since when her health has been poor and she has seldom performed.

TOMMY FLANAGAN

Tommy Flanagan was born in 1930 and like a number of significant jazz musicians of the Forties and Fifties—including his fellow pianists Hank Jones and Kenny Barron—Tommy Flanagan hails from Detroit. Like Jones, though entirely compatible with bebop in style, he also had affinities with an earlier era, especially with the poise and beautiful touch of Thirties players like Teddy Wilson and Art Tatum.

In the mid to late Fifties these virtues made Flanagan one of the most heavily recorded piano players in New York, but largely on other people's albums. During this period he appeared on Coltrane's *Giant Steps* and Rollins's *Saxophone Colossus*—two ground-breaking masterpieces—but turns up sounding just as comfortable with earlier figures like Coleman Hawkins and the idiosyncratic swing clarinettist Pee Wee Russell.

Flanagan spent most of the next decade unobtrusively accompanying the singers Tony Bennett and Ella Fitzgerald, and might have continued to do so had he not made the brave decision in the Seventies to try his luck on his own. Since then a string of duet and trio recordings have established him as one of the half-dozen or so most immaculate and inventive pianists in contemporary jazz.

ERROLL GARNER

Erroll Garner was one of the most notable and most idiosyncratic pianists in jazz history. Born in 1921 and a self-taught performer who never learnt to read a note of music, Garner came up with a style which owes little to the other developments in the jazz of his own generation. He was a two-handed "orchestral" pianist who appeared at a time when most performers were following Bud Powell's right-hand lines—and in this respect he resembled the Harlem "stride" players and Art Tatum (the latter used to refer to Garner as "my little boy"). But really, Garner—with his strange schizophrenic habit of letting his left hand lag behind the beat and wild, iconoclastic introductions to the most innocuous of tunes—did not sound much like anybody else. Nor did he play much with other performers after the early days when he made a few recordings with Charlie Parker and Wardell Gray. He spent most of his career as a solo attraction working with bass and drums—which gives a certain sameness to his output. But neither that nor his immense popularity should obscure the fact that Garner, who died in 1977, was one of the immortals of the jazz piano.

STAN GETZ

Some of the prettiest sounds ever to emerge from a saxophone came out of the tenor of the late Stan Getz—notes that sighed, and cooed, and keened; phrases that, as Dave Gelly once put it, hung in the air like wreaths of smoke. It is all there in his solo on Woody Herman's 'Early Autumn', recorded in 1948 when he was just 21, which made his reputation overnight. Of the white disciples of Lester Young, he was the most sensitive and lyrical, though without any of the Kansas City blues of the original.

After spending 1947 to 1949 with Herman, where he sat beside Zoot Sims in the saxophone section, Getz went out on his own, and quickly became one of the most celebrated soloists in jazz. The early Fifties—when he recorded prolifically, especially for Verve—was perhaps his most consistently excellent period, but he scored his two most resounding successes after returning to America from a spell in Europe between 1958 and 1961. Thereupon he made, first, *Focus* (1961), the finest of all jazz-plus-strings albums (and arguably Getz's own masterpiece), and then *Jazz Samba* (1962), which launched the jazz Bossa Nova craze and took Getz to the top of the pop charts.

Despite a long fight against cancer, he continued to play brilliantly to the end, recording some admirable duets with the pianist Kenny Barron shortly before his death in 1991.

DIZZY GILLESPIE

John Birks "Dizzy" Gillespie started out as a fiery young trumpeter at the height of the swing era. He took as his model the fastest and highest trumpeter around, Roy Eldridge. Eventually, he sounded remarkably like Eldridge, and even succeeded on occasion in out-doing his idol in speed and height of note. This, however, was not enough for Gillespie. He was searching for a new music, harmonically and rhythmically more complex than swing, which came to be known as bebop.

Born in 1917, Gillespie was one of the key figures in bop. Charlie Parker was working on similar lines in Kansas City and he was the greater improviser of the two. But Gillespie was the first to lead a bop group, and the first to organize a bop big band. He was also—more or less single-handedly—the initiator of the mixture of bop with Latin rhythm which was called cubop in the Forties and underlies the Latin jazz of today.

He was the one who publicized the new music, indeed, with his beret, clowning, nonsense singing and engaging stage manner, he was in many ways an updated version of jivy swing bandleaders like Cab Calloway (for whom he had once worked).

Arguably, his peak as a trumpeter and a recording artist was the period from the mid Fifties to the mid Sixties. He was unable to sustain the athletic aspects of his extraordinary style after that, but he remained a patriarchal presence in jazz to the end. He died in 1993.

JIMMY GIUFFRE

Jimmy Giuffre is a remarkably versatile musician, a gifted arranger and a performer who plays clarinet, almost all the saxophones, and also the flute. He is also stylistically mobile, moving from straight-ahead, swinging jazz to the area where jazz begins to blend into classical music. Born in 1921, his first big success was the roaring *Four Brothers Of '48* for Woody Herman (although his finest arrangements are perhaps to be found on the album *Lee Konitz Meets Jimmy Giuffre* of 1959). In the mid Fifties Giuffre scored a hit on his own account with 'The Train And The River', a driving railway evocation performed

The versatile arranger, composer and multi-instrumentalist Jimmy Giuffre has pursued his own brand of zen pastoralism in jazz since the fifties.

by a trio of clarinet, bass and guitar. Most of the work of the Giuffre Trio—which he had been inspired to form by hearing Debussy's 'Sonata For Flute, Viola And Harp'—was in a far more pastoral vein. The melancholy, limpid influence of French Impressionist music was still audible in the work his trio—including Paul Bley on piano and Steve Swallow on bass—of 1961. The group moved into a quasi-abstract idiom close to free jazz and modern classical music. Giuffre's career was erratic in the Sixties and Seventies, but he has returned to more prominence in recent years, recording and touring once more with Bley and Swallow.

BENNY GOODMAN

A prodigy, born in 1909, Benny Goodman was already playing clarinet around Chicago in the early Twenties (wearing short trousers). As a soloist, his career falls into two parts. First came an early phase in which he plays with the urgency and tonal roughness of other Chicago clarinettists like Frank Teschmacher. Some like this rougher, more emotional work best. But by the mid Thirties, it had been replaced by his immensely influential mature style, still forceful but technically ultra-smooth.

At this point, Goodman organized a big band based on the sound of the Fletcher Henderson Orchestra which

changed musical history. Through radio broadcasts and a celebrated tour in 1935, it set off the craze for big band swing. Goodman himself became an international celebrity. From then on, again, his work divides into two parts. There was the big band, always admirably drilled and rehearsed (Goodman was a disciplinarian of legendary unpopularity among musicians), and then—generally of more jazz interest—the small group. In this area he bravely employed black musicians in mixed groups. In 1935 he featured a trio including himself, Teddy Wilson on piano and the drummer Gene Krupa. Next the vibes player Lionel Hampton was added to make it a quartet. In 1939, the guitarist Charlie Christian appeared, plus the trumpeter Cootie Williams, who were featured in the Benny Goodman Sextet of 1940-1.

This was Goodman's musical high-water mark, but he continued to organize bands and small groups at intervals for the rest of his life. He was a perfectionist who once named "being a prize stinker" as the prime qualification for band-leading. None of his ensembles ever sounded less than excellent. Goodman died in 1986.

DEXTER GORDON

Born in 1923, Dexter Gordon was sometimes regarded as the leading tenor saxophonist in bop, but in fact, like almost all the tenor players of the Forties, he owed a lot to swing. His principal influence was Lester Young, but

Six foot six and wearing size 14 shoes, Long Tall Dexter Gordon was about the most imposing figure ever to play the tenor saxophone.

Gordon developed a much heavier tone than most of Young's disciples, something he probably derived from the other great tenor of the Thirties, Coleman Hawkins.

However, Gordon's did also incorporate a large proportion of bop elements. He also picked up an unfortunate part of the bop lifestyle—heroin addiction. For that reason he spent a large part of the Fifties in prison. Early in the Sixties, however, he made a comeback, sounding, if anything, stronger than ever. He made a series of excellent albums for Blue Note, and moved to Europe where he remained—mainly in Copenhagen—for most of the Sixties and Seventies. He returned to the States, a hero back from exile, in 1976, and died in 1989.

A huge man with a herculean constitution, he continued to live the life of a Forties hipster long after most of the others had expired. This made him a natural choice to play the lead in Tavernier's *Round Midnight* (1986), based on the lives of Lester Young and Bud Powell. By that stage, however, chronic emphysema was making it difficult for him to play, and towards the end he became musically inactive.

STEPHANE GRAPPELLI

Grappelli is not only one of the first European jazz musicians, he has also proved one of the most enduring. Born

in 1908, he came to fame as Django Reinhardt's violin playing partner in the Quintet of the Hot Club of France—he also plays piano—but he is a very different personality from Reinhardt, both personally and musically. The guitarist was a wayward, brilliant individualist; Grappelli balanced him with suavity and charm. His is a very Gallic type of jazz, quite unbluesy, but full of zest and melodic sparkle. The violinist was separated from Reinhardt by the war—which Grappelli spent in England—and subsequent efforts to reunite them were unsuccessful.

Grappelli's career has gone on from strength to strength as he becomes a grander and grander old man. In the Seventies he made a number of albums with the classical violinist Yehudi Menuhin, and he also recorded prolifically with jazzier colleagues, including George Shearing and Joe Pass.

Among his most successful partnerships is that with the British guitarist, Martin Taylor. Suave as ever, he celebrated his eighty-fifth birthday with a couple of concerts at the Barbican Hall, London, in 1993.

Stéphane Grappelli, the urbane Gallic master of the violin, has enjoyed one of the longest careers in jazz.

BOBBY HACKETT

Bobby Hackett's beautiful tone, long, elegantly embellished lines and perfectly polished phrasing made him a great favourite with fellow trumpet-players, and Dizzy Gillespie, Louis Armstrong and Miles Davis were among his admirers. But he did not always find the ideal context for his music.

When he originally appeared on the Thirties jazz scene (he had been born in 1915), he was seen as a second Beiderbecke—with justification, as at that stage he was playing cornet and using distinctly Bixian phrases. For much of the rest of his life he played with Beiderbecke's Chicagoan contemporaries, men like Eddie Condon. But Condon-style dixieland could be a trifle brash for the reflective Hackett. He sounded good with a big band, but his own effort to lead one ended in disaster. During the war, he worked with Glenn Miller, but managed only to record one utterly brilliant 12-bar solo on 'A String Of Pearls'.

In the Fifties he made a number of very successful recordings with strings, under the name of the comedian Jackie Gleason. But perhaps his finest work of the period is on a beautiful album with Jack Teagarden, *Jazz Ultimate*. In the final decade of his life Hackett found another perfectly compatible musical partner, the trombonist Vic Dickenson, with whom he made several gentle, wryly humorous albums. He played a good deal in the Cape Cod area near his home and died in 1976.

JIM HALL

Most dulcet of guitarists, Jim Hall (born in 1930) also has a good claim to be the most original performer on his instrument to appear between Django Reinhardt and Charlie Christian in the Thirties, and the advent of rock. His limpid, melodic approach makes him the Chopin, or perhaps Debussy, of the jazz guitar.

He has had a busy and varied career, on both West and East coasts. On the former, in the mid Fifties, he started out with the cool Chico Hamilton Quintet, and Jimmy Giuffre Trio. In addition, he recorded a still un-reissued album at that time with the splendidly named Modest Jazz Trio (Hall, plus the bassist Red Kelly, and Red Mitchell on piano) and made a renowned duet album—*Undercurrent*—with the pianist Bill Evans, a fellow spirit if ever there was one.

He moved to New York, and in 1962 joined—to the accompaniment of some raised eyebrows—the rumbus-tiously exploratory tenor player, Sonny Rollins. This was an odd combination, but it worked, and led to Hall's work taking a more adventurous turn. After leaving Rollins in 1964, apart from a partnership with Art Farmer, he has worked mainly in his trios and duos, with the bassist Ron Carter an especially compatible partner.

SCOTT HAMILTON

The tenor saxophonist Scott Hamilton is the most spec-tacular example of the way in which jazz history went into partial reverse in the Eighties and Nineties. Born in 1954, he appeared in New York in 1976 aged 22—in the heyday of fusion and at the tail end of the free jazz boom—as a bril-liantly persuasive performer in the manner of Thirties and early Forties.

Dashing, romantic Scott Hamilton is the Douglas Fairbanks Jr. of the tenor sax.

Hamilton rapidly made an international reputation, but initially many people's reaction was that this must be a case of artificial flowers. But as the years have gone by, that criticism has faded. Hamilton is simply too gifted a performer to be dismissed—distinctive, dynamic, bub-bling with fresh ideas. He retains an overpowering Ben Webster-like tone on ballads—each note engulfs you like a huge warm bank of sound. But otherwise he is com-ing to resemble more and more that wonderful genera-tion of tenor players who listened to both Lester Young and Charlie Parker—Wardell Gray, Al Cohn, Zoot Sims and Stan Getz, for example. He has recorded a string of albums for the Concord label, with his own Quintet—

containing fellow natives of Providence, Rhode Island in the guitarist Chris Flory and the drummer Chuck Riggs—and in many other contexts. These albums document the unfolding powers of an undeniably major saxophonist.

LIONEL HAMPTON

Hampton has the rare distinction of having introduced a brand new instrument to jazz. Early on he learned drums and piano (both of which he still plays). Around 1930, however, he discovered in the vibraharp—a metallic variant of the xylophone with an electric fan which allows notes to be sustained—the perfect medium for his talents. At up-tempos, he uses the vibes, like the drums, as a medium for infectiously forceful swing; but he is also capable of rhapsodic ballad interpretation. On occasion, Hampton also features himself playing drums, two-fingers piano, and singing.

Born in 1908, in 1936 he became a member of the Benny Goodman Quartet, and shortly afterwards began a series—like the similar one under Teddy Wilson's name—of studio recordings with small groups including many of the finest players of the period.

In 1940, Hampton launched a big band of his own, and has run one, on and off, until the present day (he last toured Europe in 1992). The Hampton big bands are noted for driving, blues-based material. Not terribly sub-

tle or innovative, they achieved great popularity with black audiences. It is a well attested fact that the Hampton theme—'Flying Home'—and his great hit from 1941—once created such excitement at the Apollo Theatre, Harlem, that the building actually began to move. In this vein, Hampton is one of the ancestors of rock 'n' roll.

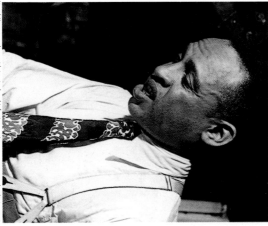

Lionel Hampton plays with inspired and infectious swing on any percussion instrument —drums, piano, but most of all the vibes which he himself introduced into jazz.

Brown, who died a decade and a half before Hargrove was born—in 1970—is a particular favourite). But Hargrove approaches this music with a confidence, and—especially in live performance—a flaring energy which carry conviction and give it a contemporary edge. He has the big tone, audacity and swaggering confidence of the really outstanding jazz soloist—reminding one at times not only of Brown, but also of Fats Navarro and the youthful Roy Eldridge. His young band is almost as impressive as its leader.

So far, in the recording studio, Hargrove has sounded a trifle restrained and over-produced—even on his excursion with Sonny Rollins on *Here's To The People* (1991). But no doubt, he will make many more records in the future. No one, in 1993, looks more like the face of the future of jazz.

COLEMAN HAWKINS

See separate entry in the Legends section.

FLETCHER HENDERSON

It was Fletcher Henderson's band, more than any other, that evolved the idiom of big band jazz. Born in 1897, black, middle class and with a chemistry degree,

ROY HARGROVE

Most of jazz history had already happened when Roy Hargrove was born in 1970. But that hasn't stopped him following in the footsteps of trumpeters like Clifford Brown. ....

The music of the latest jazz wunderkind is still more a matter of promise than achievement—particularly as far as recordings are concerned. But this trumpeter—still in his early twenties—has made more impact than any other newcomer in the last few years.

Essentially, his music is neo-classical, based on that of the bop masters of the Forties and Fifties (Clifford

Henderson drifted into music, and by 1924 found himself leading a big band at the celebrated Roseland Ballroom in Manhattan.

He comes across as a man of strange passivity. He never made a fuss about anything, and tolerated astonishing levels of drunkenness and lateness among his musicians. Partly as a consequence, his bands were seldom as successful as their musical brilliance deserved. But the roll-call of his musicians is virtually a roster of the greatest players of the Twenties and early Thirties.

In the Twenties, the arrangements were largely done by the altoist Don Redman. But Henderson's own later scores—such as 'Wrappin' It Up'—were even better: superbly elegant, brilliantly simple and easy-swinging. They provided the blueprint for the age of swing, after Henderson had sold them to Benny Goodman. He died in 1952.

JOE HENDERSON

In the Sixties the tenor saxophone was dominated by two giants—Rollins and Coltrane—and it was difficult for younger performers of the instrument to avoid those influences. But, although he was affected by both, Joe Henderson (who was born in 1937) succeeded in sounding quite individual. In particular, in contrast to the dominating strength of sound deployed by both those giants, Henderson has always had a mellower, gentler approach and an unassuming tone on the instrument.

In the early to mid Sixties Henderson was heavily recorded with Horace Silver—to whose group he belonged for a while—and various other leaders. He performed on the trumpeter Lee Morgan's infectiously swinging *The Sidewinder* (1963) and *The Rumproller* (1965), two of the jazz hits of the day, and also on McCoy Tyner's *The Real McCoy* (1967). Under his own name he made excellent recordings for Blue Note, including *Page One* (1963) and *Inner Urge*, with Tyner (1964). These were great days for Henderson, but the Seventies were not. Indeed, he was something of a forgotten figure until the appearance of two much acclaimed albums—*The State of the Tenor, Volume 1* and *Volume 2*—in 1985. In the last couple of years he has again been recorded heavily, producing, among others, a reflective album of Billy Strayhorn compositions, *Lush Life* (1992)

WOODY HERMAN

Born in 1913, Woody (Woodrow) Herman took over the Isham Jones band in 1936, but his real jazz success did not come for nearly a decade, with his band of the mid-Forties—known as the First Herd. This, while not being exactly a bebop ensemble, had something of the fiery spirit of the new music. It also had a number of outstanding members in the tenor saxophonist Flip Philips, the trombonist Bill Harris and drummer Dave Tough. This band caught something of the spirit of the

Second Herds saw Herman's greatest days, but he continued to lead very fine bands until the Sixties and they all acted as nurseries for new talent. The years before his death in 1987 were darkened by a tax dispute with the Inland Revenue Service, which claimed he owed them a six-figure sum and at one point seized his house.

EARL HINES

Hines was the most influential pianist of his day—the main line of keyboard jazz descends from him. Where he got his style from is one of the minor mysteries of jazz. All we know is that, having been in born in 1903, he popped up as a young man in Pittsburgh with a revolutionary way of approaching the piano. His bass patterns were far less regular than those of stride or ragtime—full of twists, turns and surprises. So too were the sparkling lines he played with his magical right hand.

times, and still conveys an exhilarating enthusiasm. Herman's essential achievement was to blend the more swinging side of bop with the Basie/Lunceford tradition.

He formed another band in 1947—dubbed the Second Herd—which was dominated by the saxophone section, consisting of three post-Lester Young tenor players—Stan Getz, Zoot Sims and Herbie Steward—plus Serge Chaloff on baritone. These were known, after a famous recording, as the Four Brothers. The First and

In 1928 he recorded some of the most durable of all jazz recordings with Louis Armstrong in Chicago; at the same time he was also working with the New Orleans clarinettist, Jimmy Noone, and making splendid solos like 'My Monday Date' and '57 Varieties'. In the Thirties and Forties he led a big band at the Grand Terrace in Chicago, at one stage employing both the bebop pioneers, Dizzy Gillespie and Charlie Parker.

After the war he joined Armstrong's All-Stars for a bit, then went through a thin period, before bursting out again in the Sixties. From then on he toured frequently, and made a string of dashing solo and group recordings. He played with indefatigable vim until the week before he died in 1983.

JOHNNY HODGES

Hodges was the sole major musician who modelled himself on the imperious New Orleans master, Sidney Bechet. In the early Twenties Bechet gave him lessons, and occasionally until he gave it up in the Forties, Hodges played Bechet's instrument—the difficult soprano saxophone. For the most part, however, Hodges, who was born in 1906, stuck to the alto, of which he was one of the half-dozen supreme players in jazz. And instead of Bechet's wandering life, Hodges spent almost his entire career—from 1928 to 1970—working for Duke Ellington, the only exception being the period 1951 to 1955, which he spent leading a very Ellingtonian little group of his own.

Essentially, Hodge's gifts fell into three parts, all ably employed by Ellington. There was a forcefully swinging, up-tempo Hodges, charmingly evident on the innumerable small-band tracks he made under his own name from the Thirties to the Sixties. Then, best of all, there was a luxuriant, rhapsodic aspect of Hodges, for which Billy Strayhorn—Ellington's composing partner—wrote many glorious vehicles over the years. 'Blood Count', Strayhorn's last work, is perhaps the finest of these. Hodges died of a heart attack in 1970, just as Ellington was wondering how to persuade him to take up the soprano again to play the 'Portrait of Sidney Bechet' for the New Orleans Suite.

BILLIE HOLIDAY

See separate entry in the Legends section.

ILLINOIS JACQUET

The tenor saxophonist Illinois Jacquet blew himself into jazz history in 1942, at the age of 19, with the solo he played of Lionel Hampton's recording of 'Flying Home', one of the few improvisations so inevitable-sounding that it is generally now included in the tune. That début, with its rich tone, bluesiness and energetic excitement was typical of much of Jacquet's music. In the Forties, showy playing—in effect a sort of early R&B tenor, with frenetic climaxes—rapidly made him a big name.

But there was much more to Jacquet than that. As became clear in later years, he was typical of a number of Forties musicians who were not interested in bebop, but instead continued to develop the music of the late swing period in which they grew up (other examples were the equally fine tenor players Lucky Thompson and Wardell Gray). In his maturity Jacquet became a passionate and highly intelligent interpreter of ballads and blues. In the late Eighties he organized a big band, with which he has toured Europe.

KEITH JARRETT

Jarrett is one of those musicians who begin within the world of jazz, and end up largely outside it. His starting point on piano was the exquisite Chopinesque romanticism of Bill Evans. But over the years he has inflated this to gigantic Bachian proportions, and added many other ingredients to form an eclectic stew—and in the process become immensely popular worldwide.

Born in 1945, he worked with Charles Lloyd in 1965–6 and Miles Davis in 1970–1, after which he has largely been out on his own. From the jazz point of view, probably his best music came in the Seventies, when he recorded both with an "American Quartet"—with tenor saxophonist Dewey Redman, Charlie Haden on bass and Paul Motian on drums—and with a "European Quartet" including the Norwegian saxophonist Jan Garbarek (another performer interesting in pushing jazz in the direction of classical and folk forms).

By this time, he had also begun his lengthy solo explorations. These—and particularly the Köln Concert from 1975—have many admirers. But whatever the merits of their eclecticism, which runs from Bach to country and western, in this writer's opinion they have none of the distinctive virtues of jazz.

JAMES P. JOHNSON

The acknowledged head of the New York school of stride pianists, Johnson was also a prolific and important composer. His celebrated pieces like 'Carolina Shout' were the benchmark against which other aspiring stride pianists were measured. Johnson's own style, with its precision, clarity and driving swing was the starting point for his most famous pupil, Thomas "Fats" Waller, with whom at one point he played duets.

In the Twenties and Thirties Johnson, who was born in 1891, devoted a good deal of his time to composing: among his many celebrated pieces were 'Running Wild', 'If I Could Be With You' and 'Charleston'. Like many North-Eastern jazz musicians, he was also interested in classical music, and produced several ambitious compositions in that vein, including a choral work, 'Yamecraw', and 'Symphony Harlem'.

He made piano rolls early in the Twenties and a number of band recordings towards the end of that decade. But many of his finest solo recordings came late in his life, after he had already suffered his first stroke in 1940. He made a number of excellent recording sessions in the mid Forties with Blue Note and Decca, among others, but he was incapacitated by another stroke in 1951 and did nothing more before his death in 1955.

J. J. JOHNSON

Born in 1924, J. J. Johnson more or less single-handedly translated bebop on to the slide trombone. The task was not an easy one, as the trombone is not naturally suited to the quickfire delivery of bop. Furthermore, the new music had no use for the glissandi and ripe tonal effects which played such an important part in the trombone-playing of the Thirties. None the less, Johnson achieved a mellow, post-war sound and incredibly rapid articulation, suggesting at times that he must be playing a valve instrument, or even a trumpet. He was the outstanding trombonist of the Forties.

His career has not been a smoothly triumphant one. For a time he was out of jazz, working in industry. After his return he made the recordings collected by Blue Note in *The Eminent J. J. Johnson* and appeared on the superb

Miles Davis *Walkin'* session. He then formed a two-trombone quintet with the Danish trombonist Kai Winding. The band—one of the most popular of the era—was generally known as "Jay And Kai". Since the late Fifties, his jazz work has been sporadic.

HANK JONES

The impeccable and elegant Hank Jones is a pianist much admired by fellow musicians. Few great performers have not worked with him at one time or another.

Stan Kenton's variable-quality bands were stuffed with excellent musicians.

Like his fellow pianist and fellow native of Detroit Tommy Flanagan, Hank Jones has a foot in both the bebop and the swing camps. Indeed, his splendidly poised solo playing often sounds like a heavily edited version of one of Art Tatum's solo extravaganzas.

Hank Jones is the eldest of a distinguished jazz family—his younger brothers Thad (1923–86) and Elvin (b. 1927) having made important contributions on, respectively, trumpet and drums. Hank, however, born in 1918, was the first to emerge on the New York jazz scene in the early Forties. In his day he has worked with virtually everybody, from Charlie Parker to Ella Fitzgerald, and has spent many years in recording studios.

He is a performer who has an immensely high reputation with his fellow musicians, who value his taste, effortless swing and perfection of touch. Consequently, Jones—like the comparably excellent Flanagan, Jimmy Rowles, Kenny Barron, Barry Harris and Ellis Larkins—has tended to become pigeon-holed as an accompanist. His solo and trio performances make clear, however, that he is one of the most distinguished performers in the history of jazz piano.

STAN KENTON

Few figures in jazz are as controversial as the pianist and bandleader Stan Kenton. To admirers of his music, there is nothing like it. To detractors—who were numerous—

Kenton's conception of the big band was seen as bombastic, pretentious and unswinging.

Born in 1912, Kenton first organized a band in 1940, but his period of greatest renown was during the late Forties when he was the leader of a West Coast movement towards what was called "progressive" big band jazz. This period culminated in 1950 in his formation of a 40-piece ensemble, including a full string section, which he dubbed "Innovations in Modern Music".

This was neither an economic, nor—by general consent—a musical success. But the bands which followed in the early Fifties often were. During those years, many of the best young white players in jazz passed through Kenton's ranks—including arrangers like Bill Russo and Bill Holman, the saxophonists Lee Konitz, Bill Perkins and Richie Kamuca, and the trumpeters Maynard Ferguson, Shorty Rogers and Conte Condoli. West Coast cool jazz can be seen as largely the music of ex-Kenton sidemen. Despite the frequent awfulness of the leader's ideas, the truth was that Kenton's bands could be very good. He died in 1979.

LEE KONITZ

The alto saxophonist Lee Konitz started his career in the circle of the pianist Lennie Tristano—a dissident coterie in Forties jazz. In contrast to the harmonic and rhythm experiments of bop, Tristano explored questions of line and encouraged his pupils—who also included the tenor player Warne Marsh—to play without the expressive inflections of the usual jazz tone. Konitz's early recordings were mainly made in the Tristano orbit, and included the ground-breaking performances in 1949 (under Tristano's leadership) without preset theme, chords or melody—free jazz a decade and a half ahead of its time.

Konitz's work has continued to be marked by intellectuality, although after the early Fifties an unTristano-like passion became evident. Much of his best Fifties work was done in company with fellow-Tristano acolytes like Marsh. Subsequently, he has seemed to take on all comers, excelling particularly in the intimacy of duets. One Konitz project consisted of musical dialogues with various partners including the drummer Elvin Jones and tenor saxophonist Joe Henderson; another was made up of duets with the bassist Red Mitchell, a third of unaccompanied alto. Everything Konitz has done, however, has been marked by rigour, clarity and adventurousness of thought.

JIMMY LUNCEFORD

Lunceford's was one of the most stylish black bands of the Thirties, and it was one with an unusual genesis. In 1927 Lunceford, a university graduate born in 1902, started to teach at Manassa High School, Memphis, and organized a student band. In time this became so popular that Lunceford turned professional, with his ex-pupils as the nucleus of his orchestra.

Lunceford's trademarks were a danceable two-beat rhythm, and especially well integrated section work (the sections were reputed to rehearse individually before the official rehearsals). He also had some outstanding soloists, including the altoist Willie Smith, an original Manassa student, who ranked third to Johnny Hodges and Benny Carter among swing altoists. In the trumpeter Sy Oliver, he also had an exceptional arranger.

The mid to late Thirties were Lunceford's heyday, the period when he made his best recordings. Today, in comparison with Basie or Ellington these can seem rather lightweight. But the Lunceford band had its own virtues, which made it a favourite with dancers and musicians. Lunceford himself died suddenly on tour in 1947, and the band did not long outlast him.

WYNTON MARSALIS

Admittedly he is member of a musical, and jazz playing, family—his father Ellis is a noted pianist, while his elder brother Branford (b. 1960) is a prominent tenor player, and Delfeayo (b. 1965) plays trombone. But even so Wynton Marsalis's progress to superstardom has been extraordinarily brisk.

Well before he was out of his teens (he was born in 1961), he was recording with Art Blakey. Then came a contract with Columbia and very high profile recordings both as a jazz musician and as a classical virtuoso (performing concerti by Haydn, Mozart and Hummel). Not surprisingly, all this provoked a reaction, often hostile. Marsalis was snubbed by Miles Davis on stage in 1986, and then ruthlessly criticized by him in his autobiography. Others have taken the view that Marsalis's music is all technical gloss, with no substance of emotion or originality. And it is true that Marsalis has moved from an idiom drawn from Miles Davis's Sixties work, to delve ever deeper into jazz history. Ellington, Jelly Roll Morton, Louis Armstrong—all are grist for his mill. The truth may be that Marsalis is a player of great gifts and admirable fidelity to jazz who has not yet found—like many of his contemporaries—a viable idiom of his own. There is still plenty of time for him to do so.

JACKIE MCLEAN

Jackie McLean is among the most intriguing of the generation of alto saxophonists who came after Charlie Parker. Naturally, the great man's shadow fell particularly strongly over those who played his own instrument. Many became clones. Some who didn't—like Art Pepper and Paul Desmond—looked back to swing. McLean was one of the first to look forward. In some ways, his career parallels that of Ornette Coleman with whom he was to record in 1967. But Coleman was the revolutionary outsider; McLean worked from inside bebop, step by step.

Born in 1932, in the Fifties he worked and recorded with Art Blakey, Charles Mingus and Miles Davis. But his most important achievement lies in the 20 or so albums he made for Blue Note between 1959 and 1967. From the start he had had an open, crying tone that was distinctively different from the Parker norm. During the Sixties he slowly edged towards greater harmonic and rhythmic independence. The interest in these records—*Let Freedom Ring*, for example, or *One Step Beyond* (both 1963)—lies not so much in the final destination, as in the interesting terrain between bop and absolute freedom which McLean traversed. He took up an academic post in 1973, and has been a less constant presence on the jazz scene since the Sixties. But he continues to record, latterly with his son René on tenor saxophone.

CARMEN McRAE

Despite being one of the major jazz singers, Carmen McRae was surprisingly slow to make a mark. Born in 1922, she did not record until 1954, and her real celebrity did not come until the next decade. In part this period of neglect can be attributed to her musical personality. She shares with her mentor, Billie Holiday, an ability to endow a lyric with real feeling. But where Billie was—and sounded like—a victim of life, McRae comes across as a survivor—tough, sardonic and completely unsentimental.

As the critic Gary Giddins has pointed out, her art is an example of an intelligent female sensibility at work. She is sometimes as rhythmically or harmonically audacious as Mel Tormé or Sarah Vaughan, but less obviously so (McRae is a pianist, and sometimes accompanies herself). Among her recent projects was an album of Thelonious Monk pieces, not something most singers would care to attempt. The most unschmaltzy of vocalists, she has never quite become the big star she deserves to be. But at 71 years of age, she is singing as well or better than ever—which means formidably well.

Carmen McRae is a singer with an entirely original approach. Tough, unsentimental, sometimes sardonic, but far from cold.

CHARLES MINGUS

A stormily emotional man, the bassist, bandleader and composer Charles Mingus produced stormily emotional and highly original music. A member of the bebop generation of the Forties, in many ways as a musical thinker he was a chronological misfit, looking backwards to Duke Ellington and forwards to free jazz. On bass, he was an absolute original—perhaps the only performer on that instrument ever to attain the button-holing eloquence of a great saxophonist or trumpeter.

Although he had recorded with Lionel Hampton and Charlie Parker, it was not until the mid Fifties that Mingus, born in 1922, began to produce recorded work that truly reflected his musical importance. The first great album was *Pithecanthrophus Erectus* (1956), with its title track a riotous evocation of early man. Over the next decade he explored collective improvisation, and combined bop with gospel elements in the brilliant *Better Git It In Your Soul*, and with Mexican music in *Tijuana Moods* (1957). He moved towards lengthy integrated compositions with *The Black Saint And The Sinner Lady* (1963) and the mammoth *Epitaph*, not collated and recorded until over a decade after his death in 1979.

In the early Sixties he moved close at times to free jazz, and it is there that his influence can most clearly

With various intermissions and one change of drummer, the members of the Modern Jazz Quartet have been making music collectively since the Forties.

be seen. But Mingus's music, like Ellington's and Monk's, is unique—in its voices, turbulent experimentation and restless changeability.

MODERN JAZZ QUARTET

Modern Jazz Quartet (often abbreviated to MJQ) started life in 1951 as a quartet led by the vibraharpist, Milt Jackson (b. 1923), and also including the pianist John Lewis, Percy Heath on bass and Kenny Clarke on drums. But the four members had previously constituted the rhythm section of the Dizzy Gillespie big band. Early on, however, the MJQ turned into a co-operative organization with Lewis as musical director. In 1955, Clarke was succeeded on drums by Connie Kay—the only change of personnel in the group's 40-odd-year existence.

As a pianist, Lewis is a performer with a spare, even-flowing quality which was once well described as "seam-lessly swinging". As a composer, he has shown a deeper and more persistent interest in European classical music than any other major figure in jazz.

Jackson was the first important vibes player to appear since Lionel Hampton, and for a long time the only one playing bop. While a less straightforwardly percussive performer than Hampton, he is capable of producing torrential, impassioned oratory from his unlikely trolley-like instrument. On the other hand, he also specializes in playing ballads of a ravishing delicacy.

The best music the MJQ has produced in its very long life has resulted when Lewis's European inclinations have been held in balance by the fire that Jackson derived from his childhood in the gospel church. This creative tension occurred pre-eminently at the emotional Last Concert of 1974 which marked the temporary break-up of the band. In the Eighties, however, they got together again. They still perform together from time to time, though all four pursue independent careers.

THELONIOUS MONK

Born in 1917, Thelonious Sphere Monk was one of the original beboppers at Minton's in 1941. But there was a difference between him and the others. Most bop took the form—following Parker and Gillespie—of a coruscating torrent of notes. Monk's mature style and compositions, on the other hand, were extraordinarily spare and epigrammatic. He would methodically explore a single idea—'Thelonious', for example, is built around one note, 'Misterioso' based on ascending intervals of a fourth. The results at first seemed dissonant, jagged, to the conventional ear. Now, the series of small group recordings Monk made in the late Forties for Blue Note are regarded as specimens of the jazz composer's art as perfect and as logical as Jelly Roll Morton's with the Red Hot Peppers. In between, it took both musicians and the public a long time to catch up with Monk—he was regard-

ed as esoteric, "the high priest of bop"—and consequently his career did not take off until the mid Fifties.

The idiosyncracies of his music were rooted in the quirks of his character. Monk was a very odd man. He would seldom speak, and when he did, what he said was distinctly enigmatic. It seems that for many years his mind was balanced between sanity and madness. But in the early Seventies, he became seriously ill, and made only one more appearance before his death in 1982.

JELLY ROLL MORTON

See separate entry in the Legends section.

GERRY MULLIGAN

Gerry Mulligan is one of the few major jazz musicians to have taken on the unwieldy baritone saxophone. But his early impact was more as an arranger. Born in 1927, he wrote for the Gene Krupa big band, and a number of scores for Miles Davis's epoch-making Nonet of 1948–9 (with which he also played). Since then he has continued to explore the idiom of the Davis group in a number of medium-sized ensembles and big bands. In 1992 he recorded new versions of the original Davis scores with some of the original performers.

His rise to jazz stardom came as a result of a small group—the piano-less quartet he formed in California in 1952 with Chet Baker on trumpet. This was a spritely affair, whose music combined the lyricism of Baker with the conversational ease of Mulligan himself. It was a tremendous hit, one of the bands that launched the cool, and the predecessor of a long line of Mulligan small groups which continues today. Such is Mulligan's consistency that there is sometimes a temptation to overlook him as a soloist, a tendency which is encouraged by the easy avuncular flow of his music. But while he lacks the intensity of the greatest jazz soloists, Mulligan is a player whose playing has a deeply reassuring melodic beauty.

DAVID MURRAY

The tenor saxophonist David Murray has done more than any other single musician to re-integrate the avant-garde of jazz with the mainstream and the roots. His influences are so eclectic as to be encyclopedic. As a soloist, he has been compared, with reason, to Ben Webster, Sidney Bechet and Illinois Jacquet on the one hand, and to the rebarbative free jazz tenors of the Sixties, Albert Ayler and Archie Shepp, on the other.

Born in 1955, he was brought up in the gospel church, and played R&B. As well as tenor, he also plays soprano and bass clarinet. There are moments when his compositions put

David Murray's musical roots seem as wide as jazz itself, but his own much-praised synthesis is highly individual.

one in mind of fellow jazz greats Duke Ellington, Charles Mingus and King Oliver.

Murray has played and recorded in a bewildering variety of contexts over the last 20 years—with the World Saxophone Quartet, solo, duet, with his own quartets, quintets, a wonderful octet, and a big band. On the whole his trajectory seems to have been away from the extremities of free jazz, and back into the tradition. Some of his recent offerings are scarcely discernible from the work of Webster, or Ellington's tenor, Paul Gonsalves (another favourite). But his most characteristic ploy has been to use the tartness of free jazz to refresh the music's more time-honoured idioms.

FATS NAVARRO

Fats Navarro's style was clearly derived from Gillespie's, but like Tadd Dameron's scores—many of which he performed—his solos were poised and reflective, where earlier bop was incandescent. Navarro stated his ambition as to "play a perfect melody of my own, all the chord progressions right, the melody fresh and original".

Navarro's lucid imagination and beautiful tone—fellow trumpeter Joe Newman called it a "big butter tone"—made him an important influence for young musicians. It is from Navarro, born in 1923, that the main line of post-war jazz trumpet descends via Clifford Brown. Navarro's own career, however, was appallingly short owing to the lethal combination of heroin addiction and TB which killed him in 1950.

During his heyday in the late Forties, he made a number of superb recordings under his own name, with Bud Powell, and best of all, with Tadd Dameron. With the latter, he flowered into one of the truly great jazz soloists—a musician as essential to Dameron's sound as Johnny Hodges was to Ellington's. But then Navarro lost the fat that gave him his nickname, his zoot suit hung on him as if on a skeleton, and he was quickly dead.

JIMMY NOONE

New Orleans clarinet playing is sometimes divided into two schools, the creole and the dirty. If Johnny Dodds, with his bluesy tone and punchy delivery, was the finest exponent of dirty playing, Noone was the leader of the creole faction. His tone was pure, his technique extraordinary—at one stage he studied with a classical teacher in Chicago. The contemporary clarinettist Kenny Davern has said that Noone remains the supreme exponent in jazz of fluid clarinet playing. From the fluid, virtuoso playing of Noone descends the mainstream of jazz clarinet, because he was one of the principal influences on the young Benny Goodman, who in turn influenced everyone else.

Born in 1895, Noone worked in a string of Chicago nightclubs, mostly the Apex, where he was in residence from 1926 to 1928, and also more briefly in New York. Unfortunately, although he recorded quite prolifically, he does not appear on record to such advantage as the other masters of New Orleans. He worked largely with his own bands for which he often preferred an unorthodox front line of two reeds, himself and an altoist. And sometimes he indulged a taste for oily sentimentality. The best Noone is to be found on the tracks he made in 1928, on which the brilliant pianist Earl Hines appeared, and the clarinettist can be heard engaging in a fine duet with the alto saxophonist, Doc Poston. Noone died in 1944.

ANITA O'DAY

The singer Anita O'Day is a transitional figure. Born in 1919, she began her career in the big swing band era before the war. From 1941 to 1943 she was a star of the Gene Krupa orchestra. This was the period in which she had her first hits—including a jivey duet with trumpeter Roy Eldridge, 'Let Me Off Up Town'. But even at that stage she was feeling her way beyond the conventions of the Thirties. Indeed, she has a good claim to be the first modern jazz singer. Certainly, her style was the source for June Christie and Chris Connor.

She is an erratic performer, who sometimes suffers intonation problems—her voice is not the perfect instrument possessed by a Fitzgerald or a Vaughan. But at her best she is able to combine the emotional engagement

of a Billie Holiday with an entirely modern adventurous recomposition of melodic line. She was at her peak through most of the Sixties, but her most mesmeric appearance was undoubtedly that at the Newport Jazz Festival of 1958, recorded in the film *Jazz on a Summer's Day*.

ODJB

A band of white musicians from New Orleans, calling themselves the Original Dixieland Jazz (or Jass) Band, were

The ODJB played an important role in publicizing the new music from New Orleans.

the first jazz group to record. The ODJB (as fans tended to abbreviate it) were talent-spotted by Al Jolson soon after they arrived in New York in 1916. Jolson subsequently arranged a recording date with Victor Records on March 5, 1917. One 78—'Livery Stable Blues'—sold a million copies. The ODJB and their version of "jazz" became all the rage. They, and a more watered-down, commercialized version of their music, were what Scott Fitzgerald had in mind when he coined the famous phrase "the jazz age".

The music of the ODJB catches something of the rhythmic vitality of the New Orleans style, but in a mechanical way. It offers only a caricature of the tonal inflections of Afro-American music—the farmyard braying on 'Livery Stable Blues', for example. At this distance in time, it comes across as funny hat music—a novelty—which is essentially what it was. Neither the band nor its members—cornettist Nick LaRocca, clarinettist Larry Shields, trombonist Eddie Edwards—did much of significance after the early Twenties. But they had put jazz on the map.

KING OLIVER

Joseph "King" Oliver—a tall, stout, dignified man who once worked as a butler—was the third in a regal succession of New Orleans cornettists, after "King" Bolden and Freddie "King" Keppard. He acquired his reputation in New Orleans while working with various bands, including Kid Ory's. Born in 1885, in 1919 he moved north to Chicago, where he took over the band led by Lawrence Duhe.

After playing at a number of locations, he started a long residency at the Lincoln Gardens in 1922. At this stage his group was named the Creole Jazz Band, and included the young Louis Armstrong—Oliver's protégé—on second cornet. In 1923-4, with this ensemble, Oliver made the first important recordings by a black jazz band.

These rather dimly recorded acoustic sides are still considered the classic examples of New Orleans jazz. Obviously, King Oliver was a great leader, but he was also an important performer in his own right, subtle and driving. His climactic muted solo on 'Dippermouth Blues', recorded in 1923, remains elating nearly 70 years after it was first played. Among other achievements, Oliver seems to have perfected the art of using mutes.

His day did not last for long. The recordings he made with his Dixie Syncopators in 1926-8 show him gamely, but not altogether successfully, trying to keep up with the new fashion for big band jazz. By this time, his own playing was deteriorating because of gum disease, fatal for a brass-player. By the end of the Twenties, his tooth-trouble was so bad that often he could scarcely play, and many of the cornet solos on his later recordings were played by somebody else. After leading a series of increasingly obscure bands, he became stranded in Savannah, Georgia, where he worked as a pool-room attendant and died almost destitute in 1938.

KID ORY

Born in 1886, Kid Ory was the dean of New Orleans trombonists, and, in 1922, also the leader of the first black jazz band to record. The trombone had a closely defined role in New Orleans jazz. The cornet or trumpet carried the melody, or lead. The clarinet decorated in the upper register, while the trombone filled in a bass line below. This trombone style was known as "tailgate" because when a band played on a cart, the trombonist sat at the back so that his slide didn't get in anyone's way. It was a choppy, driving, limited idiom, and in it Ory excelled.

He was the trombonist on Louis Armstrong's *Hot Fives* and *Sevens*, and on Morton's *Red Hot Pepper* sides. He played with Oliver and Dodds. In Twenties Chicago he seemed to be everywhere. When the bad times came for New Orleans jazz musicians in the Thirties, he ran a chicken farm, returning with the New Orleans revival of the Forties. At this stage he played again with Armstrong and appeared in the film *New Orleans*. Through the trad boom of the Fifties, he led a series of sometimes rough but always spirited bands. Retired from 1966, he died in 1973.

CHARLIE PARKER

See separate entry in the Legends section.

ART PEPPER

Horror is a natural response to the life of the reed-player Art Pepper. As we learn from his autobiography, *Straight Life*, he was a slave to drugs of all kinds—heroin, of course, but at one stage even cough mixture. He spent the Fifties in and out of gaol for various escapades, including bank robbery; and most of the Sixties and early Seventies behind bars.

In photographs, the young and old Pepper confront each other like Dorian Gray and his portrait—the one clean-cut and all-American, the other a grotesquely tattooed old con.

Under the circumstances it is surprising that Pepper, born in 1925, managed to record any worthwhile music at all. In fact he did a lot. The early recordings for Contemporary are uniformly superb, most of all *Art Pepper Meets The Rhythm Section* (1957)—one of the exemplary albums of the decade—but also *Smack Up*, *Gettin' Together*, *Intensity* (all 1960), and several others.

His tone on the alto saxophone—his principal instrument, although he also performed brilliantly on clarinet and tenor—had the airiness of Lester Young, but also a passionate cutting edge. His ideas flowed with extraordinary lucidity.

The music Pepper made after his return to jazz in 1973 showed the influence of John Coltrane and has its admirers. But in the view of this writer, Pepper was no longer the player he had been in his youth. He died in 1982.

OSCAR PETERSON

The Canadian pianist Oscar Peterson, born in 1925, belongs chronologically to the post-war jazz world, but his style has little to do with bebop. Possessed of an astonishingly fluent technique—he has been described as the Liszt of jazz—he is actually one of the line of virtuoso keyboard individualists which also includes Erroll Garner and Art Tatum. Early influences included Garner, George Shearing and (particularly) Nat King Cole. Later on he listened to Tatum. In general—like Cole and Garner, unlike Tatum in his early years—Peterson has preferred to work with a trio, sometimes bass and drums, sometimes bass and guitar. The most famous of these was the Fifties line-up with bassist Ray Brown and Herb Ellis on guitar.

Early on Peterson became, and has remained, one of the most popular musicians in jazz. As a recording artist he has been astoundingly prolific, especially for the impresario Norman Granz. In the Fifties, he was virtually house-pianist for Verve records; in the Seventies and Eighties he worked busily again for Granz's new Pablo label. This ubiquity and the garrulousness of Peterson's approach has led some critics to become impatient with him, but—while perhaps not the most profound of piano players—he is a remarkably amiable and consistent performer.

BUD POWELL

Born in 1924, Bud Powell was the basic influence on jazz piano during the Forties. Basing himself partly on Art Tatum, Powell developed a style of quicksilver lines and fiery virtuosity. At times it suggested a translation of Charlie Parker's alto saxophone improvisations to the keyboard, and especially the pianist's right hand.

Powell was also one of the saddest cases in jazz of a talent marred by illness. Whether because of a beating inflicted by the police in 1944, abuse of drink and drugs, or inherent instability, Powell's behaviour was erratic almost from the start.

When he was on form, especially in the Forties and early Fifties, he could play with ferocity, blinding speed and pell-mell invention like nothing else in piano jazz. But when he was down, as he probably often was as a result of drink or sedation, he sounded bewildered. His work in the Fifties was increasingly patchy, although sometimes still magnificent. In 1959 he moved to Paris where he was befriended and nurtured by a young fan, Francis Paudras (their relationship was the basis of the Tavernier film *Round Midnight*). He died in 1966.

DJANGO REINHARDT

The guitarist Django Reinhardt was the first great jazz musician to come out of Europe; indeed, until the Sixties he was the only one. He accomplished this despite having lost the use of two fingers on his left hand in a caravan fire, and not having heard American jazz until around 1931. In effect, he blended the music of his people, of which he was already a virtuoso, with the idiom of Americans like Armstrong and Venuti. The result was individual and magnificent.

Born in 1910, he was a member of the charming Quintet of the Hot Club of France with Stephane Grappelli on violin. With this group he made many of his finest records between its foundation in 1934 and the Second World War, which he spent trapped in Paris. In the late Thirties Reinhardt also made a number of wonderful records with visiting Americans, including Coleman Hawkins, Benny Carter and the trombonist Dicky Wells.

During the war Reinhardt was a symbol of bohemian resistance to the Nazis, and became hugely famous. As a gypsy, he was a candidate for a concentration camp,

Gipsy guitarist Django Reinhardt was one of jazz's charismatic performers.

but led a charmed life. Musically, his decline started in the Forties. After the war he took up amplified guitar—which proved to be a mistake. A tour of America in 1947 was a disaster. His career was in the doldrums when he died of a stroke aged 43 in 1953.

BUDDY RICH

One of the great virtuosos of jazz, the drummer Buddy Rich was a performer whose imagination was not always the equal of his technique. None the less, at his best Rich was excellent, and an important bandleader. Born in 1917, he began as an infant prodigy, playing on Broadway under the name "Infant Taps" at the age of 4. A notable showman, Rich played with many of the major swing bandleaders in the Thirties and early Forties—Tommy Dorsey, Bunny Berigan, Benny Carter, Harry James and Artie Shaw. In the Fifties he became a prolific recording artist on Norman Granz's Verve label. Sometimes he was in context, as with the trumpeter Harry Edison, and in an astonishing trio of the three biggest show-offs in jazz with Lionel Hampton and Art Tatum. On occasion, as with Charlie Parker and Dizzy Gillespie, his straight-ahead swing was less appropriate.

In the late Sixties he went right against the trend of the times and formed a roaring big band, reforming again in 1975. Despite heart by-pass surgery, he continued touring intensively into the mid-Eighties. He died in 1987.

MAX ROACH

Born in 1924, Max Roach was not the first bebop drummer, but on the whole he was the most influential—a performer whose lucid handling of the rhythmic complexities of the new music was matched by a crystalline sound on the drum kit. Having worked with Charlie Parker and Miles Davis in the Forties, his career as a leader began when he formed a quintet with the trumpeter Clifford Brown in 1954. This was one of the great jazz groups of all time, and the next couple of years constituted Roach's golden era. During that time he recorded outstanding music not only with Brown, but also with Sonny Rollins, the tenor player with the Quintet.

The death of Brown and the band's pianist, Ritchie Powell, in a car accident came as a devastating blow to Roach. He continued to lead bands of a similar type throughout the Fifties, but not until he found the trumpeter Booker Little (1938–61) did he find a collaborator of anything like Brown's quality. Sadly, Little too died cruelly young—at the age of 23.

In the Sixties Roach's interests turned to politics—a development expressed in *We Insist—Freedom Now!* (1960), which featured the voice of his wife Abbey Lincoln. As time went on, he also became associated with the free jazz movement. His latter-day enterprises have included M'Boom, a percussion ensemble, the Max Roach Double Quartet, which incorporates an all-female string quartet, and several choral works.

SONNY ROLLINS

In the mid Fifties after Charlie Parker's death no one came closer than Rollins to matching the musical power and creativity of bebop's lost leader. Rollins, however, played tenor, and played it in a new-sounding way—more chunky than Forties tenors, with fewer chromatic runs and more thematic exploration. With this hard-boiled emotional attitude, there went a new sort of instrumental sound—rough, tough, overwhelmingly strong, and an approach to a ballad that was as likely to be sardonic as romantic.

In the mid to late Fifties he produced a stream of extraordinarily high-quality recordings for a number of different companies, including *Saxophone Colossus* for Prestige, *A Night At The Village Vanguard* for Blue Note and *Way Out West* for Prestige. Then, just as Ornette Coleman and John Coltrane appeared on the scene with radically new approaches to improvisation, Rollins (born in 1929) disappeared for a long sabbatical.

After a couple of years of thought, practice and body building, he returned to jazz in 1962—but without a fresh breakthrough to offer the world. In the Sixties he toyed on occasion with the styles of Coleman and Coltrane, but more often stuck to his own musical language. In the late Sixties, he took another break—and came back again to flirt more seriously with free jazz and fusion. This time, however, the great recordings were much fewer—if there were any. In recent years he has again moved closer to the idiom of the Fifties. He remains today the single most overwhelmingly impressive improviser in jazz, but he is a colossus who continues to have difficulty in making albums which truly reflect his talent.

JIMMY ROWLES

Over the years, Jimmy, born in 1918, has made innumerable albums as an accompanist to Billy Holiday, Ben Webster, Zoot Sims, Benny Carter and Bob Brookmeyer, so much so that he was pegged—like Ellis Larkins and Hank Jones—as the perfect pianist in the background, especially for lady singers. But he is much more than this. His thistledown touch, Whistlerian shading of notes, Rolex precision of timing and impish imagination make him one of the most beguiling pianists in post-war jazz.

In the Fifties he recorded a great deal, but largely in other people's bands. And for many years the practically lived in the Los Angeles television and recording studios (he was the vocal coach who taught Marilyn Monroe to sing). Then, in the early Seventies, he broke out, moved to New York and devoted the next decade full-time to jazz. From this period dates some of the finest Rowles on record— among the best of all, his two collaborations with the bass-player Ray Brown, and another set of duets with the tenor saxophonist, Al Cohn. Since his return to California, less has been heard from Rowles, but he continues to record on occasion.

GEORGE RUSSELL

George Russell is an experimental musical highbrow—but one who dances as he directs his big band, seeming to form arcane sonic spaces in the air with his hands.
....
Born in 1923, the composer and bandleader George Russell was perhaps the most radical jazz composer of the Forties, issuing scores at infrequent intervals like revolutionary manifestos—in 1947 *Cubano Be, Cubano Bop* for Dizzy Gillespie, *A Bird In Igor's Yard* (whose name gives

the clue to two of Russell's sources—Parker and Stravinsky) in 1949. Then in 1953 came his theoretical credo in the form of a book, *The Lydian Chromatic Concept Of Tonal Organization*. This introduced the idea of improvisation on modes (scales) rather than chords, a notion which Miles Davis latched on to and made one of the most influential devices in the jazz of the last 30 years.

Russell's ideas take some digesting, and perhaps it's not surprising that his career has been a stop-and-start affair, dotted with periods of silence and sojourns in academia. But in the Fifties and early Sixties he produced a series of brilliant, sometimes rather cerebral albums.

From 1964 he spent a good deal of time in Scandinavia, where he worked with the Norwegian saxophonist Jan Garbarek. Russell quickly embraced the sounds of rock, and this electrification gives his work of the Seventies and Eighties a new punch. In the last decade he has received more of the recognition he deserves.

PEE WEE RUSSELL

Russell was one of jazz's most notable musical eccentrics, as well as a supreme clarinetist. His approach to the clarinet took the "dirty" style to an anarchic extreme. In Russell solos of the Thirties and Forties, his clarinet grunts, shrieks, rasps and approaches the theme with a harmonic *laissez-faire* unheard of at the time. And he looked as odd as he sounded, a tall, thin man with drooping shoulders and a moustachioed, long-nosed face somewhere between George Orwell's and Schnozzle Durante's.

Russell recorded early on with Coleman Hawkins and Henry Allen—the latter was an equally idiosyncratic fellow spirit, and their recordings are among the most hell-for-leather in existence. But he was mainly associated with the white Chicagoan traditionalists. Throughout the Thirties and Forties Russell was a mainstay of Eddie Condon's groups and recorded numerous sides with them. But after a serious illness in 1950, brought on by alcoholism, he cut loose from Condon-style dixieland.

In the Fifties and Sixties he often worked with more modern musicians, at one stage with a pianoless quartet performing compositions by Coltrane, Monk and Ornette Coleman. The playing of his later years could be as gentle and diaphanous—sometimes a note seems no more than saliva and a sigh—as his early work was ferocious.

DAVID SANBORN

The alto and soprano saxophonist David Sanborn is one of the few real stars of the jazz world—able to fill the major classic arenas. One reason why—which strikes you immediately—is that Sanborn has a strong, beautiful, expressive tone on his instrument. Its sound is obviously derived from the blues, which was his starting point.

Born in 1945, he suffered from polio as a child and took up wind-playing for therapeutic reasons. In his early teens he was already playing with bluesmen like Albert King. In 1967 he joined the Paul Butterfield Blues Band, then went on to play with Gil Evans—and also the Brecker Brothers, plus non-jazz figures like Stevie Wonder, David Bowie and Paul Simon.

There is no doubt that at his best Sanborn is a player of considerable power. He is one of the major performers to come out of jazz-fusion and funk. The trouble with a significant number of his bands and recordings is that often nothing much is done with the splendid noise he makes, except to wrap it up in unmemorable packaging. Too often, beneath the undoubted bluesiness, there is only blandness.

The aching intensity of the blues fires the music of the influential saxophonist David Sanborn, one of the icons of Seventies and Eighties jazz.

ARTIE SHAW

A firebrand and a maverick, Shaw was in some ways the most interesting of the swing bandleaders. He repeatedly gave up show-business in favour of other activities — farming was one, novel-writing another. His private life was sensational: among his eight wives were Ava Gardner and Lana Turner. But his music was more reflective than all that hell-raising might suggest.

As a clarinettist, Shaw was an inventive improviser and extremely assured technician, without having the exciting edge of a hot jazz man like Pee Wee Russell, while as a leader Shaw was a pioneer in blending jazz and classical idioms. He first made an impression by appearing with a string quartet at a swing concert. In 1940, when he was an established star, he put together a band consisting of a conventional 15-piece swing line-up, plus woodwinds and strings.

This unusual angle made his ensembles less stereotyped than most of the swing era (he also employed some excellent musicians, including the great trumpeters Roy Eldridge and Hot Lips Page). In the long run, however, Shaw, born in 1910, became bored with leading swing bands. He last played the clarinet in public in 1954, although he still makes appearances as a conductor.

Hollywood good looks and film star wives were part of the popular allure of Artie Shaw, but he was — and is — a more interesting musician than that might suggest.

ARCHIE SHEPP

The career of tenor saxophonist Archie Shepp has been a barometer of changing moods in jazz from the Sixties to the Nineties. Born in 1937, he first emerged as a scion of the avant-garde, recording with Cecil Taylor, and later with John Coltrane in his free jazz phase. His predominant influence, however, was probably Ornette Coleman. At this stage, few players made a more explicit connection between radical jazz and the emerging rhetoric of the black power movement—for example on *Fire Music* (1965). But even then, other influences were apparent—Rollins, Ben Webster, the bluesy Texan tenors like Illinois Jacquet. Beneath the anger, there was romanticism (Shepp has remarked that he is worse than a romantic: "I'm a sentimentalist", he says).

By the Eighties, the latter aspect was evidently on top. Shepp's African robes were replaced by three-piece suits. And, though avant-gardisms were still apparent, his playing came more and more to resemble a blurred version of Webster, Jacquet, or—on alto—Charlie Parker. On occasion, he sings the blues, and has worked in recent years with the admirable bluesy pianist Horace Parlan. This incarnation is undoubtedly easier on the ear. But those who can digest the asperities of his earlier work will probably find it more significant.

WAYNE SHORTER

Born in 1933, Wayne Shorter was the most promising tenor saxophonist to appear in the immediate wake of Sonny Rollins and John Coltrane. His work of the early to mid Sixties was certainly indebted to those two looming titans—as was that of all his contemporaries—but Shorter's conception was distinctly different. The clearest way of putting this is to say that Shorter thought like a composer, giving each of his solos a comprehensible structure. And indeed, at this time his work as a composer was as important as his saxophone improvisations.

He played a great part in shaping Art Blakey's Jazz Messengers between 1959 and 1963 (arguably the Messengers' finest period). To that period belong most of his best compositions, classic pieces like 'Lester Left Town', 'Ping-Pong' and 'Chess Players'.

He joined Miles Davis in 1964 and stayed until 1970, forming a worthy sparring partner for Davis in the classic quintet of the mid Sixties (with Herbie Hancock on piano and Tony Williams on drums). At this time he also made a number of distinguished albums under his own name for Blue Note, including *Speak No Evil* (1964) and *Adam's Apple* (1966).

Subsequently he pursued the jazz-rock line that Davis had begun, founding Weather Report with the keyboard player, Joe Zawinul. This was the most popular of all rock-fusion bands, lasting until 1986, but the thinking behind it was increasingly Zawinul's.

HORACE SILVER

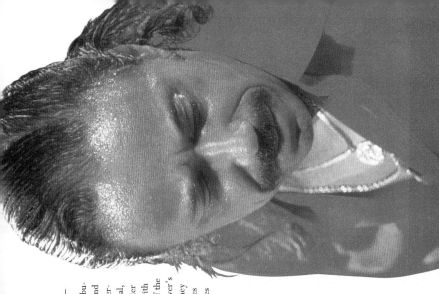

As a soloist, the pianist Horace Silver's contribution was to take Bud Powell's bebop style and simplify it, bluesify it, and render it more percussive. The result proved immensely influential, but Silver's influence was perhaps even greater as a bandleader and composer. Silver divides with Art Blakey the title of the outstanding leader of the hard bop movement. Indeed, Blakey and Silver's efforts are not entirely separable since they worked together from 1954 to 1956, sometimes under Blakey's nominal leadership, sometimes under Silver's.

From the latter date, however, Silver, who was born in 1928, led his own quintets, and his work as a composer was strongly emphasized. 'The Preacher', an early piece of Silver, helped set the fashion for bop that reached back to its gospel roots. Through the Fifties and Sixties, Silver's bands continued to exploit this vein of catchy danceable music—what came to be called funk—and in consequence were not only musically excellent, but highly popular. A couple of albums—*Song for my Father* (1965) and *Cape Verdean Blues* (1966)—made the charts. Silver's work demonstrates that jazz can be accessible and fun. His bands also—like Blakey's—served as a finishing school for

Horace Silver's brand of bop is rhythmically insistent and melodically catchy—in a word, fun—his bands were among the most popular of the Fifties and Sixties.

young players (including the trumpeters Carmell Jones and Blue Mitchell, and tenor saxophonist Joe Henderson). His recordings since the Sixties, however, have been sparse and less interesting.

ZOOT SIMS

John Haley Sims, known as Zoot and born in 1925, was a pre-eminent example of those musicians who make no startling innovation, but continue and nourish the jazz tradition by playing superbly and being unmistakably themselves. Originally, he was one of the flood of young white tenor saxophonists who appeared in the Forties, taking Lester Young as their point of departure. Sims, like Stan Getz, was a member of the Woody Herman saxophone section from 1947 to 1949—all disciples of Lester—known from a famous recording as the Four Brothers.

Even at that stage Sims was the most directly swinging of the four. Later on, an irresistible buoyant swing became the

Sims trademark. In the Fifties he formed a musical partnership with another Lester Youngish tenor player, Al Cohn (1925—88). The two were extremely compatible (Cohn was another ex-Herman player), and worked together intermittently for decades. Towards the end of his life, Sims's playing attained a rich and mellow maturity, exhibited on a series of admirable albums on the Pablo label. On some of the best of these he was accompanied by the pianist Jimmy Rowles. He played with warmth and passion until the night before he died in 1985.

BESSIE SMITH

The greatest of the so-called classic blues singers, Bessie Smith was perhaps not strictly a jazz performer. But she worked with many jazz musicians, influenced others, and through the scale of her success affected the history of jazz itself. She was born in Chattanooga, Tennessee, in 1894, but little is known of her early life. Around 1912 she started touring with the Rabbit Foot Minstrels. By the end of the decade she was a big enough name to tour with her own troupe. Then in 1923 came her big break—a recording session.

There was already a fashion for blues, but previous records had been distinctly genteel. Bessie was by far the earthiest, most authentic black singer to have been recorded, and the elation and indomitable strength with which she sang 'Down Hearted Blues' made it a huge hit. In consequence the recording companies discovered a new market for genuine black music, and Bessie became a star.

Over the following few years she made many beautiful sides with accompanists such as Louis Armstrong, James P. Johnson and the lyrical cornettist Joe Smith, but by the end of the Twenties, her music had gone out of fashion, and Bessie was down on her luck—not helped by her truculent behaviour when drunk. She recorded again in 1933, and, like other Twenties performers, would doubtless have returned to favour if she had not been killed in a car accident outside Clarksdale, Mississippi, in 1937.

ART TATUM

Born in 1909, the pianist Art Tatum was one of the most extraordinary virtuosi that any form of music has produced in this century. His starting point was Fats Waller's stride. "Fats", he once said, "that's where I come out of—and, man, that's quite a place to come from". But he quickly left stride behind. His mature style was based on prodigiously rich embellishment of the theme—doublings and halvings of the tempo, unbelievably fast and even runs, every sort of harmonic variation and enrichment. All of which was perhaps even more phenomenal in that he was virtually blind from an early age. Tatum's technique astonished classical masters such as Horowitz, and amazed his fellow jazz pianists even more.

Blind pianist Art Tatum never saw a note of music, but that did not prevent him becoming one of the most astonishing virtuosi of the century.

To this day no one has equalled him. Essentially, his work changed little from his first recordings (in 1933) to his last, although a live club performance from the Forties found him looser and more informal than usual. Most of the time he worked as a soloist, though in the mid Forties he had a successful trio with Slam Stewart on bass and Tiny Grimes on guitar. Tatum's playing was invariably impeccable, but his greatest monument was the 13 solo and eight group albums he made for Verve towards the end of his life. He died in 1956.

CECIL TAYLOR

The pianist Cecil Taylor has produced some of the most uncompromisingly difficult music in the jazz canon. He was, with Ornette Coleman, the most important forerunner of free jazz to appear in the Fifties, but their respective idioms are very different. Coleman's is basically straightforward and relatively accessible; Taylor's improvisations are dense, complex, orchestral and often furiously energetic. His performances can last for much longer than the average jazz piece, or even jazz set, sometimes for over an hour. He has a reputation for wrecking pianos, and for much of his career inadvertently exhausted and alienated audiences.

His early recorded work from the mid Fifties was very radical for the times, but he did not reach full impassioned maturity for another decade—the moment signalled by two Blue Note albums, *Unit Structures* and *Conquistador*, both 1966. At this stage, and for many years afterwards, Taylor had difficulty in finding regular work in the US. His most solid following was, and probably still is, in Europe, where in 1988, during a festival devoted to his music in Berlin, he made a monumental series of solo and group recordings on the FMP label.

Taylor, born in 1930, continues to divide listeners. Some find him a great master, others can't stand him. But he is undeniably one of the most extraordinary figures in jazz.

JACK TEAGARDEN

Teagarden made the trombone—hitherto a trifle clumsy—a voice as melodically fluent as the trumpet of Armstrong or cornet of Beiderbecke. This gliding ease, together with a noble sadness, are the defining properties of his music. Although a white musician of German extraction (born in 1905), he excelled in that quintessentially black idiom, the blues. Teagarden was also one of the finest of jazz singers: in the same class as Armstrong. When singing he had a lazy, drawled, slightly slurred delivery which is highly distinctive. As a vocalist, he sounds inspired, but slightly drunk, which, as it happens, he often was.

In the late Twenties and early Thirties—his golden period—he appeared on numerous recording sessions with colleagues like Eddie Condon, Louis Armstrong and Benny Goodman. During the mid Thirties he worked for the musically dull Paul Whiteman Orchestra, then tried to lead big bands of his own, with results which were musically mixed and financially disastrous. Subsequently, he spent some time with Louis Armstrong's All Stars. Perhaps the most successful recording of this period was the album *Jazz Ultimate*, which he made with Bobby Hackett in 1957. Arguably, he was the greatest of all jazz trombonists; certainly, he ranks with the great black performers Jimmy Harrison, Vic Dickenson and Dickie Wells. Teagarden died in 1964.

CLARK TERRY

In his suite 'A Drum Is A Woman', Duke Ellington cast the trumpeter and flugelhornist Clark Terry, born in 1920, as the spirit of bebop, but in many ways he belongs in the earlier world of swing. Terry, in fact, is one of those musicians who occupies the border territory between the two styles. In just the same way, in the chronology of St Louis trumpeters, Terry fits in between the definitely mainstream Shorty Baker and Miles Davis .

It is possible to argue that there was a distinct St Louis school of brass players, certainly all those three listed above were characterized by mellowness of tone and lack of vibrato. Terry, in addition, possesses a remarkable bubbling facility on his two instruments (in the Shakespearean suite, Ellington not unnaturally cast him as Puck).

Much of Terry's career was spent in big bands—Hampton, Basie and, most significantly, Ellington from 1951 to 1959 (a period he refers to as the University of Ellingtonia). Thereafter, in the Sixties, he co-led a quintet with the trombonist Bob Brookmeyer, and occasionally a big band.

Mercurial and mellow-toned, the sound of Clark Terry's trumpet has been admired by his fellow instrumentalists from Miles Davis to Wynton Marsalis.

In the Nineties he remains an active figure on the New York jazz scene, and something of a father—or grandfather—figure to young trumpeters like Wynton Marsalis.

MEL TORMÉ

Mel Tormé is not only a jazz singer. He is also one of the classic American popular vocalists—a few years ago Frank Sinatra classified him with himself and Tony Bennett as the only "real saloon singers" left. Tormé's work does not belong entirely within the borders of jazz: his recordings from his crooning heyday in the Forties—the era when he was dubbed "the velvet fog"—for example, do not. But he has a remarkable affinity with jazz, a fact probably traceable to his early enthusiasm for the music (his boyhood idol was Buddy Rich, and he is a proficient percussionist in the Rich style).

Some of his greatest recordings were achieved in the Fifties with a light and limber ten-piece jazz band led by the arranger Marty Paich, into which Tormé's voice was integrated just as if it had been a trumpet or a saxophone. He can phrase with the rhythmic deftness of a jazz drummer, and the melodic sure-footedness of a saxophonist.

Born in 1925 and now in his sixties, Tormé retains remarkable vocal powers—a smooth yet engaging husky tone that does indeed suggest mist and velvet, range,

accuracy, stamina. In the Eighties he has issued a number of quite outstanding albums, including a Grammy award-winner made in partnership with the pianist George Shearing.

McCOY TYNER

One of the key pianists of the Sixties, Tyner, born in 1938, came to prominence as a member of the classic John Coltrane Quartet. His approach to the keyboard is chunkily two-handed and orchestral. At times his music's sheer weight renders it unwieldy; at others it creates an exciting momentum or luxuriant romanticism. In contrast to the out and out freedom of a Cecil Taylor, Tyner's work remained within harmonic and metrical limits—though sometimes only just.

Tyner came to musical maturity while he was with Coltrane, and much of his best work dates from the mid to late Sixties period—shortly after he left the Coltrane group in 1965—when he was recording for the Blue Note label. At this stage, most of his albums were with medium sized bands involving a number of horns—among the very best being *The Real McCoy* (1967), a collaboration with the tenor saxophonist Joe Henderson, with his old Coltrane Quartet colleague, Elvin Jones on drums. Latterly, he has frequently worked with a trio, but also recorded solo albums and one with a big band.

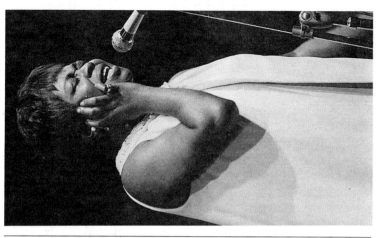

SARAH VAUGHAN

Born in 1924, Sarah Vaughan was a controversial figure. To some listeners—including some important musicians—she was simply the greatest of all jazz singers, with an unparalleled technique. Others thought her an example of too much coloratura, and too little taste. Without much doubt, however, she was the most significant jazz vocalist to emerge in the Forties. She performed in the Billy Eckstine and Earl Hines bands beside Charlie Parker and Dizzy Gillespie, and was capable of harmonic adventurousness analogous to theirs.

Although she recorded in the Forties, her best work came later—as did many albums of lesser interest. In general, the better the company, the better she was. Her finest hour, in the opinion of many admirers, came on the album she made with the trumpeter Clifford Brown in 1954. Other excellent work resulted from meetings in the studio with the Basie band, and the guitarist Mundell Lowe. The Sixties were a less glorious decade, but Vaughan was very much on form for the albums she made in the Seventies and early Eighties for the Pablo label with such collaborators as Oscar Peterson and Joe Pass. At her worst she was capable of overripe and rather aimless embellishment of a song; at her best, she made some of the most sumptuously beautiful sounds jazz has ever known. She died in 1990.

Joe Venuti

One of the first and best jazz violinists, Giuseppi Venuti came of an immigrant Italian family in Philadelphia. He was born in 1903. In the mid Twenties he moved to New York and formed a musical partnership with the guitarist Eddie Lang, also of Italian extraction. During this period he played with a number of bands, including Paul Whiteman's, where he was a colleague of Bix Beiderbecke and Bing Crosby.

But his greatest triumphs came in the recording studio on the numerous splendid pieces of chamber jazz he made with Lang. There were duets, Venuti's Blue Four, and various combinations with the leading white musicians of the day, including Beiderbecke, Teagarden and the young Benny Goodman. During those days, Venuti also laid the foundations of his reputation as the leading practical joker in jazz. Putting jello in Bix Beiderbecke's bath was one of the milder of his pranks.

Lang died in 1933, and Venuti did little of significance between the mid Thirties and late Sixties, for some of which time he was handicapped by alcoholism. But he enjoyed an extraordinary late flowering, making a string of records on which his leading characteristics—lyrical tenderness, ferocious swing and wild humour, mixed in equal measures—are displayed even better than before.

Fats Waller

Thomas "Fats" Waller was one of the most irresistible entertainers of the century, a singer, composer and comedian of effervescent ability. He was also a jazz pianist of great talent—talent some jazz writers have been sad he did not put to better use. Born in 1904, the son of a church minister, he spent the rest of his life rebelling in bohemian fashion against his respectable, God-fearing family. He ate and drank sensational quantities, enough to cause his early death in 1943 at the age of 39.

Waller was the pupil of James P. Johnson, and one of the greatest pianists of the Harlem stride school. Indeed, it is arguable that he outdid his master in solos like 'Numb Fumblin', 'Handful of Keys', and 'Alligator Crawl'. He also learnt the organ in his youth, and continued to record on it—sometimes to rather lugubrious effect—throughout his career. Waller made a number of excellent solo and small band recordings in the Twenties and early Thirties. But his greatest success did not start until 1934 when he began recording and touring with a regular band, Fats Waller And His Rhythm.

The Rhythm sides—of which there are hundreds—are mainly devoted to tin-pan alley ephemera, often mercilessly guyed by Waller. But they all swing, and the best of them rank among the most euphoric jazz on record.

BEN WEBSTER

Around 1934 the lead trumpeter of Fletcher Henderson's band gave the tenor saxophonist some good advice. "You've got a nice little tone there", he said to Ben Webster. "Why don't you work on it?" And work on it Ben did, until in time it became one of the glories of jazz—soft, warm, huge and extraordinarily beautiful.

Born in 1909, Webster hailed from Kansas City, and was a friend and contemporary of Lester Young. By jazz standards, however, he matured quite late, not really coming into his own until he joined Duke Ellington in 1939. Webster was one of the key members of the superb Ellington band of the early Forties, and Duke exploited both his sensuous way with a ballad and the spirited, not to say ferocious, way he tackled up-tempo pieces like the celebrated 'Cottontail'.

Arguably, however, Webster did not find his absolute top form until the Fifties and early Sixties, by which time he was the equal of his old hero, Coleman Hawkins. During this period, in fact, Webster recorded a couple of albums with Hawkins—neither giving an inch—and made other splendid recordings with Oscar Peterson, Sweets Edison and Billie Holiday. He moved to Copenhagen in 1964, and thereafter his music lost a little of the old magic. Webster died in 1973.

TEDDY WILSON

Born in 1912, Teddy Wilson was the leading piano stylist of the Thirties (Art Tatum excepted), and he performed in a fashion which has been described as "Earl Hines without the surprises". That is not entirely fair, since Wilson's music had a fastidious, slightly melancholy elegance all his own. But Hines was his starting point. Wilson came to fame as the pianist in the Benny Goodman Trio of 1935. In the same year he began a lengthy and glorious series of studio recordings under his own name which featured most of the great musicians of the era—most frequently of all, the young Billie Holiday. This was Wilson's great period. In 1939 he left Goodman, led a big band of his own which failed to take off, and for the next 6 years led a sextet in New York.

Wilson was still playing with tremendous style and brio in the Fifties, especially on trio sessions with the drummer Jo Jones, and with Lester Young on the Verve label. But in the last couple of decades of his life (he died in 1986), his music—though never less than delightful—lost a degree of engagement.

Teddy Wilson was one of the most elegant keyboard performers in jazz. His music—suave, swinging, neatly melodic—was the epitome of Thirties style.

WOODS

A precocious musician, Woods, born in 1931, was performing competent alto saxophone in the manner of Charlie Parker at the age of 16. But he soon developed an urbane bitter-sweet sound of his own perhaps owing something to Benny Carter (the relationship becomes clearer on the rare occasions Woods plays clarinet).

In the Fifties and early Sixties he was a busy man on the New York scene, recording with Monk and Quincy Jones, and mainstreamers like Carter and Coleman Hawkins. For a while he co-led a quintet with fellow alto saxophonist Gene Quill—the twin alto front-line working surprisingly well.

In the later Sixties, he tended to drop out of sight, and finally moved to Europe—where he seemed to lose his way for a while, flirting with electric jazz, and then undergoing the influence of Coltrane and Rollins. He returned to the States, where just as bop has undergone a resurgence, so has Woods. His Quintet has been one of the most consistent and successful acoustic bebop groups of the last decade.

LESTER YOUNG

See separate entry in the Legends section.

LOUIS ARMSTRONG

Satchmo the Great

✳✳✳

Trumpeter/Singer
Born: August 4, 1901, New Orleans, USA
Died: July 6, 1971, New York City, USA

Possibly Louis Armstrong was illegitimate; it is quite likely that his mother was a part-time prostitute. His father deserted the family shortly after Louis's birth in 1901. As a boy, Armstrong went barefoot and lived in the red-light district of New Orleans—an area catering for working-class black customers where knifings, shootings and vice in every form were commonplace.

It was an upbringing as deprived as in any ghetto of today, apart from the rich musical culture that surrounded him. At the age of 11 or 12, Armstrong was committed by a court to the Coloured Waifs' Home, a sort of reformatory-cum-charity school. There he joined the band, and got some rudimentary instruction on cornet (the favoured instrument of military bands, and universal among early jazz musicians until Armstrong himself switched to trumpet in the late Twenties).

He left determined to become a professional player, and by 1919 he was working in Kid Ory's band, the best in New Orleans. In 1922 he was summoned to Chicago to play second cornet in King Oliver's Creole Jazz Band. Within 5 years he had transformed jazz; within 10 he was one of the most

legends

famous performers in the world. How did he do it? Although Armstrong spawned many new ideas, he did not gain this prominence through a specific innovation. It was the sheer quality of his playing that made the difference. Essentially, he demonstrated the potential of the jazz solo with such conviction and imaginative power that the music became forthwith what it has subsequently remained — a soloist's art. Other players were moving in the same direction. But Armstrong's example was simply overwhelming. For the next generation he became, in the words of Ruby Braff, "a musical university and a universe of music".

One can follow the process on the records. He plays brief but already distinctive solos on a few of the King Oliver records from 1923, notably 'Riverside Blues' and 'Tears.' In spite of the dim acoustic recording it is clear that he had already begun to develop his marvellous instrumental sound — rich yet urgent, rounded even in the upper register.

In 1925 he embarked on the series of recordings with his Hot Five (sometimes augmented to Hot Seven) which are among the great glories of jazz. Four years later, having engaged Earl Hines as pianist and produced 'West End Blues' — generally acknowledged as his masterpiece — he moved back to New York,

and rapidly became a star entertainer rather than a pure jazz musician. By the early Thirties he was fronting a big band and touring Europe. Singing took an increasingly important part in his work. The process had begun by which he became Satchmo, the grinning international celebrity, performer of 'Hello Dolly', and 'Wonderful World', who died full of fame and honours in 1971.

To the jazz fan, this has always seemed a sell-out, but that judgement is not entirely fair. For one thing, Armstrong continued at times to produce wonderful music right up to the early Sixties. Much of his big band work from the Thirties is superb; and it was at this time that he had his greatest impact as a singer. Armstrong's singing was of great importance for popular music in general, because he sang as he played, with the same rhythmic and harmonic freedom and willingness to recast the melody — and this set off a vocal revolution. Without Armstrong, neither Crosby, nor Sinatra, nor, for that matter, Elvis Presley, would have sounded as they did.

ORNETTE COLEMAN

Prophet of Freedom

* * *

Alto and Tenor Saxophonist/Violinist/Trumpeter
Born: March 19, 1930, Fort Worth, Texas, USA

WHEN THE ALTO SAXOPHONIST ORNETTE COLEMAN FIRST HIT JAZZ HEADLINES IN THE LATE FIFTIES, OPINION WAS EVENLY DIVIDED AS TO WHETHER HE WAS A GENIUS OR A CHARLATAN. A LOT OF PEOPLE THOUGHT THAT HIS MUSIC WAS THE FIRST REALLY NEW APPROACH IN JAZZ SINCE BEBOP IN THE FORTIES OR, AS AN EARLY COLEMAN ALBUM TITLE PUT IT, *THE SHAPE OF JAZZ TO COME*.

On the other hand, a lot of other people, including some very hip ones, suspected that Coleman's unusual sense of pitch and strange sense of harmony sprang from pretension, or sheer incompetence. "Trouble is," the bassist Charles Mingus hurtfully remarked, "he can't play it straight."

But, three decades on, there isn't much doubt that Coleman is an important musician (even Mingus changed his mind). The free jazz movement of which he was the prime progenitor achieved some successes (as well as a lot of screaming, freaked-out excesses) in the Sixties, and still persists, generally in a less aggressive form, today. But his music never quite became the accepted musical language in the way the innovations of Dizzy Gillespie and Charlie Parker once did. In fact, in the Nineties a bright young soloist is more likely to pop up playing bebop than Ornette Coleman-style.

Incomprehension between himself and his audience dogged the early stages of Coleman's career. He was born and brought up in Fort Worth, Texas—blues territory. But from the first he heard harmony in a different way from other people. He upset people—once he was beaten up and his alto saxophone broken. In the Fifties he moved to California, where he adopted the long hair and sandals of a pre-hippy. There he continued to be thrown off band stands, but in time he attracted a few followers, in particular the trumpeter Don Cherry. In 1958 he attracted the attention of John Lewis and Percy Heath of the MJQ, and recorded two albums. By 1959 Coleman and Cherry, plus Charlie Haden on bass and Billy Higgins on drums, were the controversial sensation of the New York jazz world.

Coleman's most easily assimilated music came in a string of quartet albums for Atlantic over the next few years, among them the audacious, some would say incoherent, *Free Jazz* (1960) by a double quartet (one in each channel). After the early Sixties, he worked more sporadically, largely because he demanded very high fees.

In 1972, he composed a work in 21 sections in which his quartet was accompanied by the London Symphony Orchestra. A few years later, in 1976, he formed a rock fusion band, Prime Time, in which his own playing is set against very loud electric accompaniment, and from this group have come a number of notable players, including the drummer Ronald Shannon Jackson and the bassist Jamaaladeen Tacuma.

Along the way he came up with a word to describe what he was doing. The word was "harmolodic" (a contraction of harmony, movement and melody), and it has spread more darkness than light. At times, Coleman himself has stated that it means "all parts are equal" (while being in different keys).

In fact, Coleman's music is not, except on very rare occasions, completely arhythmically, aharmonically, unmelodically free. It obeys rules of its own, but rules which are very hard to formulate. In some

ways Coleman is old-fashioned. Aspects of his style seem to come out of the Texan R&B bands he grew up in, and before that to some primordial Afro-American country music. It's easy enough to describe the elements in the mix — the refreshingly tart quarter-tone pitch, the spry rhythmic bounce, the direct bluesy emotion that comes across in instrumental shouts and sighs. But how to reduce all this to a recipe?

Coleman's harmolodics may not be the broad highway down which

the whole world is ever going to swing. But himself is one of those intransigently individual players whose confidence in themselves somehow convinces the listener too.

JOHN COLTRANE

A Love Supreme

* * *

Tenor and Soprano Saxophonist
Born: September 23, 1926, Hamlet, North Carolina, USA
Died: July 17, 1967, New York City, USA

THE TENOR SAXOPHONIST JOHN COLTRANE HAS HAD AN EFFECT ON THE JAZZ OF THE LAST 30 YEARS EQUALLED ONLY BY ONE OTHER MUSICIAN—HIS ONE-TIME EMPLOYER, MILES DAVIS. BUT DAVIS'S INFLUENCE WAS MAINLY ON GROUP STYLES AS RELATIVELY FEW MUSICIANS IMITATED HIS IDIOSYNCRATIC TRUMPET STYLE. COLTRANE'S DISCIPLES—AND CLONES—HAVE BEEN NUMBERLESS.

In the Seventies, indeed, it was difficult to find a young saxophonist who had *not* been influenced by 'trane. In this respect, his effect has been as all-pervading as Louis Armstrong's and Charlie Parker's were before him.

Unlike those two, however, Coltrane was a relatively late starter. Dogged by drug addiction and alcoholism, he spent his twenties in a motley array of bands, including bluesy R&B outfits and a mainstream group led by the alto saxophonist Johnny Hodges. He was approaching 30 before he first made a real impact—when he joined the Miles Davis Quintet in 1955.

His function in this, the outstanding jazz ensemble of its day, was to act as a foil to the leader. Davis's trumpet was lyrical, spare, his lines carefully edited. Coltrane, in contrast, was extraordinarily voluble on his instrument, as he was bent on taking the harmonic explorations of bebop to their logi-

cal extreme, which meant playing every possible permutation of every chord before going on to the next one. The result was a jet-stream of notes and long solos. "I can't stop playing," he once told Miles Davis, who occasionally found his star tenor player irritating. "Try taking the horn out of your mouth," Davis replied.

In addition, Coltrane had a remarkable sound, not like Lester Young, Coleman Hawkins, Parker or Sonny Rollins (the normal models). His tone was intense, hard and pure, owing, just conceivably, something to Hodges, who was in turn influenced by the proud crow of the New Orleans master, Sidney Bechet.

In 1957, Coltrane left the Davis band and forced himself to give up drink and drugs—which he did, for ever. But from now on his compulsions—apart from sweets—were musical. In the same year he played an important gig at the 5 Spot in New York with the pianist Thelonious Monk. It is probable that the extreme sparseness of Monk's accompaniment—sometimes he

John Coltrane spent his short life searching for a new style of jazz.

would not play at all for many bars—encouraged the saxophonist towards ever more independent musical explorations. *Giant Steps* (1959), his best album to date,

hypnotic, eastern atmosphere. This performance ran to 13 minutes; a later live version lasted 45 minutes.

In 1960, Coltrane formed his classic quartet with Jimmy Garrison on

summed up Coltrane's achievements of the Fifties, and seemed infinitely.

'My Favourite Things' (1960) showed the way forward in two ways. First, it unveiled his soprano saxophone style—the first successful use of this difficult instrument since Sidney Bechet. Second, it had a hit in the modal treatment of 'My Favourite Things' with its

bass, the drummer Elvin Jones, weaving complex polyrhythms, and the pianist McCoy Tyner see-sawing between chords in a way that enabled the saxophone line to expand indefinitely—sometimes it seemed infinitely.

To enthusiasts, half-hour Coltrane solos were virtually mystical experiences. And spirituality, it was increasingly clear, was the direction in which Coltrane himself was heading. This tendency led in 1964 to *A Love Supreme*—seen by many as Coltrane's masterpiece—with its unison chants and section titles like 'Pursuance' and 'Psalm'.

His final manner was based on the free jazz of younger men like Albert Ayler and Archie Shepp, and was played with new companions—his second wife Alice, the tenor player Pharoah Saunders and drummer Rashid Ali. For some, these final works are the culmination of Coltrane's work; for others, they are chaotic failures. However, it seems appropriate that after he died of liver cancer in 1967 an esoteric religious cult was founded in his memory.

MILES DAVIS

The Prince of Darkness

Trumpeter
Born: May 25, 1926, Alton, Illinois, USA
Died: September 28, 1991, Santa Monica,
California, USA

MILES DAVIS HAD A VAST IMPACT ON JAZZ—AND BEYOND JAZZ—FROM THE FORTIES TO THE NINETIES. AND HE DID SO DESPITE THE FACT THAT, ALMOST ALONE AMONG MAJOR JAZZ INFLUENCES, HE DID NOT HAVE VIRTUOSO COMMAND OF HIS INSTRUMENT, THE TRUMPET.

His work sometimes faltered; there were wrong notes; he was incapable of the speed or acrobatic flights of Dizzy Gillespie. What he had was a steely musical intelligence and a completely original idea of how he wanted to sound. In addition to that individual, unforgettable sound, his contribution to jazz took the form of a series of highly influential ideas.

His career was made up of a number of distinct phases. First, the early years, starting from the point at which Charlie Parker selected him—a shy 20-year-old from a wealthy black family in St Louis—as his musical partner for his quintet of 1947–8. Davis's clouded tone and pared-down approach owed as much to earlier masters of lyrical jazz like Billie Holiday and Lester Young as it did to bop. And he carried this emphasis of tonal beauty and melody in his first great experiment—the Miles Davis Nonet of 1948.

This was an ensemble an entirely novel kind—light, suave, neither a big band nor a small group. It only existed for the span of one short engage-

ment and a few recording sessions, but it heralded the next phase of jazz, a reaction against the heat and complexity of bop—the cool.

Davis's own fortunes plunged in the early Fifties, when he was afflicted with heroin addiction. By the mid Fifties, however, he had recovered and reached musical maturity. There was lyricism still in his playing, but also pent-up anger and brooding melancholy, especially when he used a harmon mute, as he generally did on ballads. As a musician, and also as a man, he was magnetic.

For the rest of his life, much of Davis's formidable musical intelligence was devoted to finding appropriate settings for his own wonderful, but potentially rather static, trumpet. In 1956 he came up with a quintet, and just as Parker had selected him as a contrast to his own business, Davis selected John Coltrane as his front-line partner, whose "dry unplaned sound", wrote Whitney Balliett of the *New Yorker*, set "Davis off like a rough mounting for a fine stone". This Miles Davis Quintet, which also had Philly

Joe Jones on drums, was one of the great jazz groups of all time. Meanwhile Davis continued to explore the idiom of his Forties Nonet in company with arranger Gil Evans. *Miles Ahead* (1957) and *Porgy And Bess* (1958) are the most successful amalgamations of jazz solo and large ensemble outside Ellington. But later Davis–Evans collaborations—*Sketches Of Spain* and *Quiet Night*—tended to veer dangerously close to sub-classical easy listening.

In 1958, however, Davis formed a sextet including Coltrane, as well as the altoist Cannonball Adderley and the white pianist Bill Evans. With this band Davis made a couple of albums—*Miles Stones* and *Kind Of Blue*—that turned jazz around.

With *Kind Of Blue* Davis reached a peak he never scaled again, although he put together another very celebrated band in the mid Sixties, with Wayne Shorter on tenor, Herbie Hancock on piano and Tony Williams on drums. But this kind of rather abstract jazz was losing its public by the end of the Sixties and Davis decided that something had to be done.

His solution was to blend his music with the newly ascendant rock, thus in effect inventing jazz-rock fusion. Here the crucial album was *Bitches Brew* (1969), which launched yet another new phase, with yet more famous names graduating from Davis's groups, and which made Davis more famous than ever.

In 1976, worn out, Davis retired for several years, which were given over, according to his autobiography, to sex and drugs. He returned in 1981, and continued to work in the fusion vein. The albums had become slicker, sometimes synthesized disco. Miles, however, remained curiously unchanged, despite the drastic alterations in backing, vastly popular to the end, in 1991.

DUKE ELLINGTON

Aristocrat of Big Band Jazz

Pianist/Composer/Bandleader
Born: April 29, 1899, Washington DC, USA
Died: May 24, 1974, New York City, USA

Edward Kennedy "Duke" Ellington was born of a middle-class black family in Washington. At first he inclined towards art as a career. But he drifted into music, and by the mid Twenties he found himself the leader of a group called the Washingtonians in a New York club.

Duke Ellington was highly intelligent, good-looking, flamboyant, witty, suave and tremendously self-confident (hence the nickname). Temperamentally, he liked to find his own way to do things—novel voicings, strange harmonies—on the basis that if it sounded good to him, it was good. Thus from an early stage his music manifested a powerful unorthodoxy. By the late Twenties he had worked out an entirely novel approach to big band jazz. Ellington used musicians—their distinctive sounds, their styles—like different colours on a canvas. By the early Thirties he had built up a whole palette of contrasted musicians—the fluid clarinettist Barney Bigard, the mellifluous alto saxophonist Johnny Hodges, the trumpeter Cootie Williams, trombonists Joe "Tricky Sam" Nanton and Laurence Brown, and Harry Carney on baritone saxophone.

Ellington composed—if that is the word—through these men. He would sometimes write down notes, but at other times take a phrase one of his men had played and put it in a certain context, or just tell the musician in words the kind of thing he wanted. Rex Stewart, a cornettist who worked with the band, left a description of Ellington at work in the Thirties: "Duke called to Hodges, 'Hey Rabbit, give me a long slow glissando against that progression. Yeah! That's it!' Next he said to Cootie Williams, 'Hey, Coots, you come in in the second bar, in a subtle manner growling softly like a little lion cub that wants his dinner but can't find his mother. Try that, okay?'"

By using such methods—part conventional composer, part Svengali, part casting director—he was able to make music that incorporated jazz musicians into a larger whole. And that larger whole was stamped with the personality of Ellington. He reinvented the art of jazz composition.

For the length of a 78 rpm record, he was able to sustain a

Duke Ellington's real instrument was his orchestra: no one ever got more beautiful sounds from a big band.

106

single mood, not just as in Armstrong's 'West End Blues' on one instrument, but with a 15- or 16-piece band. Thus 'Mood Indigo', from 1930, is an eery jazz nocturn, quite different from the clashing drama of 'Ko Ko,' his masterpiece from 1940, or the sensual grace of 'Warm Valley', his exquisite vehicle for Johnny Hodges from the same year.

Broadcasting every night from the Cotton Club in Harlem, where Ellington's band was a mainstay for several years, he

and his band rapidly became famous. In 1933, they crossed the Atlantic to Europe, and discovered that they were already celebrities overseas. Ellington's renown was established long before the swing band craze of the late Thirties, and carried on long after. Many people feel that Ellington reached his absolute peak between 1939 and 1942, a period when his splendid team of the Twenties and Thirties had been augmented by two further brilliant musicians—the rich-toned tenor saxophonist Ben Webster, and the short-lived Jimmy Blanton (1918–42), a frail young man who invented the art of modern bass playing. But there is much to be said for the band of the late Twenties, and also that of the late Fifties, including a new set of star Ellingtonians like the trumpeter Clark Terry and the tenor player Paul Gonsalves. It was the latter band who produced Duke's wonderful Shakespearian

suite, 'Such Sweet Thunder' (1957). Unlike so many jazz musicians, Ellington did not flower for a few years, then decline, but made excellent music for half a century.

Musicians came and went—only Carney stayed with him from first to last—but Duke went on. Ellington music was a collaborative venture. Many of his most famous tunes, on closer examination, turn out to have been dreamed up by band members. From the Forties to the Sixties, he collaborated on most projects with the gifted composer/arranger Billy Strayhorn (1915–67). But the controlling taste was Ellington's. He left vast quantities of music, by far the most imposing body of work in jazz. Some of his ambitious post-war projects, especially the Sacred Concerts, tend to be diffuse and pretentious in parts. But almost nothing he did is without moments of glory, and his contribution was immense. Miles Davis once suggested that all musicians should set aside a day sometime to say thank you to Duke.

COLEMAN HAWKINS

Father of the Tenor Saxophone

Tenor Saxophonist
Born: November 21, 1904, St Joseph, Missouri, USA
Died: May 19, 1969, New York City, USA

I N THE LAST FOUR DECADES, THE PRINCIPAL INSTRUMENT OF JAZZ HAS COME TO BE THE TENOR SAXOPHONE. BUT THAT WAS NOT ALWAYS THE CASE. THE SAXOPHONE HAD LITTLE PLACE IN THE CLASSICAL NEW ORLEANS BAND.

Indeed, apart from military bands this newcomer to the family of instruments—it had been invented only in 1840—played little part in music of any kind. A few jazz pioneers took up saxophone in the Twenties. A few performed jazz on tenor before Hawkins, but it was overwhelmingly his example which put the instrument in the dominant position it has today.

His family were secure and relatively prosperous. Encouraged by his mother, he studied music from an early age, and took up first cello, then saxophone, eventually fixing on the tenor version. A life-long listener to classical music of all kinds, Hawkins had a much better grasp of conventional musical theory than Louis Armstrong and the New Orleans masters. On the other hand, he lacked the others' early immersion in the jazz and blues traditions.

A precocious and talented player, Hawkins rapidly gained a place in the New York music business. And by 1924, when Armstrong arrived, he was already installed as the star of the Fletcher Henderson band. At that stage

Armstrong showed him the potential that lay in the solo but Hawkins was a very different player. Where Armstrong was, above all else, a melodist, Hawkins's style was built on rhythmic drive combined with a very sophisticated employment of harmony, the product of his contact with European music.

His mature style did not emerge until 1929 on two sides made under the leadership of Red McKenzie, an up-tempo piece called 'Hallo Lola', and a luxuriant ballad, 'One Hour'. These set the two basic modes of Hawkins's playing. On fast numbers, his playing surged forward with tremendous force and a multiplicity of notes, often arranged in harmonic runs or arpeggios; at slower tempos he became sensuous and rhapsodic. On both he employed a magnificently rich tone—rough at up-tempo, with velvety strength on ballads. The invention of the jazz ballad perhaps constitutes Hawkins's most important single contribution.

He continued to refine this manner as star soloist of the Henderson band until 1934, when he moved to

Europe. The next 5 years were spent in England and France; in the latter in 1938 he recorded some extraordinary music with the guitarist Django Reinhardt and a fellow American, the alto saxophonist Benny Carter. On his return to the USA in 1939, at the age of 35, he had attained the status of an old master. Soon afterwards, he made his recorded masterpiece, 'Body and Soul', which thereafter has set the standard for jazz ballad playing.

It is characteristic of Hawkins that he did not become set in his ways. On the contrary, he got better and better and moved with the times. Connoisseurs of his work consider the mid 1940s one of his most fruitful periods. Of all the older players, Hawkins was one of the most well disposed to the bebop revolution—by 1944 he was employing the bebop pianist Thelonious Monk in his band—and, always advanced in this respect, he had little trouble with bop harmony. Rhythmically, however, he remained a swing man. Like his contemporaries, Hawkins was out of the limelight in the late

Forties and early Fifties while bop and cool were all the rage. But by the late Fifties he was again recording abundantly, and in some ways sounding better than ever, with titanic strength of tone and incredible force of delivery. A young player complained at this time to another tenor saxophonist that playing next to Hawkins frightened him. "Coleman Hawkins", he was told, *"is supposed to frighten you."*

His music did not decline until the last few years of his life, during which, beset by melancholia and ever-heavier drinking, he virtually starved himself to death. He was said to

live on several bottles of brandy a day and one Chinese meal a week. Growing his hair and beard, he started to shuffle like an old man. Quite why he did all this is not clear. Always a hard man, tough on his musical rivals, granitic in his timbre, he ended by being strangely hard on himself. He died in 1969.

Tenor saxophonist Coleman Hawkins

BILLIE HOLIDAY

Lady Day

* * *

Singer

Born: April 7, 1915, Baltimore, Maryland, USA
Died: July 17, 1959, New York City, USA

IN RETROSPECT, BILLIE HOLIDAY (1915-59) SEEMS LIKE A FATED VICTIM. HER FAMILY BACKGROUND WAS APPALLING, AS IS SUGGESTED BY THE MEMORABLE FIRST SENTENCE OF HER AUTOBIOGRAPHY, *LADY SINGS THE BLUES*. "MOM AND POP WERE JUST A COUPLE OF KIDS WHEN THEY GOT MARRIED.

He was eighteen, she was sixteen, and I was three." Her father, a noted jazz guitarist, soon abandoned the family; her mother worked as a maid. Billie also worked as a maid, then found her way into teenage prostitution and served a short prison sentence before discovering that she could work as a singer.

Billie's first recordings were made in 1933, with a Benny Goodman band, and by then her distinctive style was already forming. It derived from Louis Armstrong's singing style (she quoted him and Bessie Smith as her models). In Satchmo's manner she would recast a melody, and often improve it, cutting it so that it draped just right across the beat. Like Armstrong, and the tenor saxophonist Lester Young, she had a way of lagging behind the rhythm section, then suddenly accelerating. But the emotional content of her music—and of course the smoky timbre of her voice—were quite different from Armstrong's breezy extroversion. More than any other singer in jazz, or pop-

ular music, she was able to inject genuine emotion into even the tritest of songs. That is to say, she was a past-mistress of the art of interpreting a lyric, shifting, emphasizing, and inflecting each phrase so that it rang absolutely true. Or as her accompanist, Mal Waldron, once put it, "she sure had a way with words".

Her work divides into three periods. In the Thirties she made dozens of sides with small jazz groups under Teddy Wilson's leadership or her own. These, made for the new juke-box market, took current pop songs, and, often against the odds, turned them into brilliant jazz. Some of the best of these feature Young, whose feeling and phrasing are so close to hers that on sides like 'Me, Myself and I', or 'He's Funny That Way' (both 1938) they sound like two voices of one person. In the mid to late Forties she recorded with a string section, and made impressive if not terribly jazzy recordings. This was her vocal peak, reached on superb Decca sides like 'Loverman' (1945), and her own composition, 'Don't Explain' (1946).

Nobody wrung more meaning from lyrics than Billie.

By the Fifties, her voice was going, possibly because of the drink and heroin addiction that killed her, equally possibly just because it was one of those known in classical music as "unhealthy". If anything, however, her ability to read a lyric was enhanced; from that point of view the sessions she made for Verve in the early to mid Fifties are among the best things she did. The very late recordings, particularly 'Lady In Satin' (1958), however croaky, are tremendously moving.

It is possible to overdo the pathos of Billie's life. In her Thirties heyday, she struck people as big, strong, beautiful and exuberantly full of life. It is far from accurate to imagine her performances as morbid. Often, even quite late on, they are funny, ironic, zestful, positively cheery. Contrary to the title of her book, she seldom sang the blues.

But there remains something terribly sad about her fate. The essential trouble, no doubt deriving from her awful childhood, was a disastrous incompetence in forming relationships. Her husbands and male companions were awful. In the early Forties, one of them introduced her to heroin, and from then on there was no escape. She was arrested in 1947, and spent 18 months in a federal reformatory. After her release she slipped back again into addiction. In the Fifties, she was drinking heavily as well: Jimmy Rowles, for some years her accompanist, reports that she had drunk a bottle of gin before making the rehearsal tape later released as *Songs and Conversations*. Whether it was the drink, the drugs or the misery that killed her, it is hard to say. But—an unbearably macabre touch—on her death bed in 1959 she was once again put under arrest on a narcotics charge.

JELLY ROLL MORTON

Mr Jelly Lord

* * *

Pianist/Composer/Singer/Bandleader
Born: October 20, 1890, New Orleans, USA
Died: July 10, 1941, Los Angeles, USA

HE PIANIST FERDINAND "JELLY ROLL" MORTON ONCE CLAIMED TO HAVE INVENTED JAZZ. HE DIDN'T QUITE DO THAT, BUT HE WAS CERTAINLY THE FIRST TO FORM THIS STRANGE NEW MUSIC WITH A COMPOSER'S HAND.

He came from a low middle-class New Orleans creole family, of which he was the black sheep. As a boy he played guitar and trombone with marching bands in street parades, before taking up piano. In time he became one of the ragtime piano "professors" who performed in higher-class gambling joints and bordellos. These men were dandies, individualists and loners. They earned far more than band musicians, partly as a result of the tips they received from champagne-swilling customers, and they considered themselves to be in an altogether higher league.

Morton, who famously wore a diamond in his front tooth, was very much a product of this flashy, corrupt and fascinating milieu. One of his *pièces de résistance* was the 'Naked Dance', written to accompany the titillating shows which the girls put on in establishments like Miss Lulu White's Mahogany Hall. At some stages in his career he attempted—probably not very successfully—to support himself by pool-sharking and pimping. He had the indefatigable gabbiness of a tent-show medicine salesman.

But unlike the other ragtime professors, Morton had a great love for the fledgling jazz he heard as he was growing up, and his ability to play low-down blues—popular with the girls—may have helped his success in the lucrative world of the bordellos. One of his last recordings was 'Mamie's Blues' (1939), which he introduces as "no doubt the first blues I heard in my life", and sings beautifully—sounding roughly as Humphrey Bogart might have done had he taken to blues singing.

Like many of the best New Orleans players, Jelly was a wanderer who left his native city early. He worked along the Gulf Coast and spent several years in California, before ending up in Chicago in the early Twenties. It is at this point that he enters recorded jazz history. He recorded as a soloist (although the best solos he made came in the late Thirties, just before he died), and with various groups. But his greatest contribution to jazz, however, is contained in a series of records he made with a group he called the Red Hot Peppers in 1926.

Morton was more than just a bandleader. He didn't override the personalities of his musicians, who included Kid Ory, the leading New Orleans trombonist, and the clarinettist Omer Simeon, but every moment of the Red Hot Peppers music was shaped by one sensibility, Morton's own. One sign of this is constant variety. On these performances—'Dr Jazz', 'Jungle Blues', 'Black Bottom Stomp' and 'The Chant' are among the finest—neither rhythm, texture, nor instrumentation remains the same for long. On these recordings Morton

emerges as the first master of the subtle art of jazz composition. He was the forerunner of Duke Ellington, Charles Mingus and Thelonious Monk, none of whom ever excelled Morton's achievements with the Red Hot Peppers .

Jelly's heyday was brief. He moved to New York, but didn't make a success of things there. There were more good recordings later in the Twenties, including some marvellous ones with just drums, piano and clarinet, a format which Benny Goodman subsequently took up. But by the mid Thirties,

Jelly Roll was a boastful man, but he backed his claims with genuine accomplishments.

Jelly was forgotten and living—possibly slightly crazy—in obscurity in Washington. Infuriated to hear his own composition 'King Porter Stomp' become a hit for Benny Goodman, he wrote his famous letter to the press, insisting that he, and no one else, had invented this jazz. Subsequently, in 1938, he was rediscovered by Alan Lomax of the Library of Congress for whom he spoke and played a marathon recorded autobiography. This, though not always strictly truthful, is among the most captivating documents in jazz, and the basis for Lomax's book *Mr Jelly Lord*. He also made some excellent recordings for Commodore and Victor, but time was running out. After a desperate drive across the USA chasing an inheritance he thought he was being cheated of, Morton died in Los Angeles in 1941, convinced he was cursed by his voodoo godmother.

Morton was touched with genius—part con man, part Walter Mitty, part musical perfectionist.

CHARLIE PARKER

Bird Gets the Worm

✳

Alto Saxophonist
Born: August 20, 1920, Kansas City, USA
Died: March 12, 1955, New York City, USA

THE BEBOP REVOLUTION OF THE FORTIES WAS NOT THE WORK OF A SINGLE MUSICIAN. MANY MADE CONTRIBUTIONS TO THE NEW HARMONIC AND RHYTHMIC LANGUAGE, NOTABLY THE TRUMPETER DIZZY GILLESPIE AND THE PIANIST THELONIOUS MONK.

BUT IT WAS THE ALTO SAXOPHONIST CHARLIE PARKER WHO MADE THE KEY CONTRIBUTION TO BOP PHRASING—THE WAY TO PUT IT ALL TOGETHER INTO A NOVEL MUSICAL LANGUAGE. AND, OUT OF THEM ALL, PARKER WAS THE IMPROVISING GENIUS.

Charlie Parker was thus one of the most significant figures in the history of jazz. Like Armstrong, he came from a broken home—brought up by his devoted mother in Kansas City, one of the key spots in jazz. The young Parker longed to emulate the great musicians who played night and day in the bars and clubs of his native town. When very young, legend has it, he was too musically ignorant to keep up and was hustled off stage. But then he set himself to study, learning Lester Young solos note for note at first. By the late Thirties, when in his late teens, he was already the star of the Jay McShann Orchestra, the best band in KC after Basie had gone. Sadly he was also already,

as he remained for the rest of his life, a junkie.

When he first came to New York Parker was, by all accounts, close in ideas to the beboppers, but he was playing with an emotional brio and rhythmic compulsion which came from the South-Western blues tradition. This is one of secrets of Parker's greatness. He was a magnificent blues player, with the same western rooster crow in his sound as a singer like Big Joe Turner. Even when Parker was not playing the blues, this feeling came through. If he played a ballad like Laura, another saxophonist once said, he played the Laura blues. This gave an emotional density to all his work.

He began his recording career with McShann in 1939, and those early tracks catch him in a transitional stage, harmonically and rhythmically advanced for swing, but not yet playing bop. At some time between 1940 and 1944, when he next recorded, Parker found out how to play the music he could hear in his head. It was all there by the time he recorded with Gillespie in

1944 and 1945. 'Ko-Ko', from the latter year, contains the first fully fledged Parker masterpiece, an unbelievably swift excursion on the chords of 'Cherokee', "Yardbird" or "Bird", the nickname he was given by other musicians, was very apt. Parker flew.

From then on, little changed. He went to the West coast in 1946, where he had a drug-induced breakdown, and spent sometime in the Camarillo State mental hospital. On returning to New York, he was briefly a little more clean-living, and made in 1947 and 1948 some of his best work.

By the end of the decade he was more strung out than ever, his weight ballooning up, his behaviour increasingly erratic. As well as being the king of bop, Parker was also the ultimate hipster. Heroin aside, he drank more, ate more, slept less, and with more women than three men put together. If his Verve recordings of the Fifties are often less impressive than his earlier work, it is because he was put in less appro-

priate contexts. To this period belong his recordings with strings, which many musicians consider his finest work.

By this time he was already more legend than man. There was something uncanny about Parker. Once he had read an arrangement, he knew it by heart and never had to look at it again. For hours on end, he would play chorus after chorus after chorus at blinding speed, all filled with brilliant, fresh ideas. Charming to some, fiendish to others, by turns sly, aggressive, mean, generous, outgoing, withdrawn—the only common factor which emerges is the

changeability of his personality. When he died at the age of 34, his body was worn out by every kind of excess. The doctor estimated his age at 60. Parker lived at a faster pace than most men, experimenting with life just as he did with notes.

Charlie Parker experimented with life, as with music.

LESTER YOUNG

President of All Tenor saxophonists

Tenor Saxophonist/Clarinettist
Born: August 27, 1909, Woodville, Mississippi, USA
Died: March 15, 1959, New York City, USA

LESTER YOUNG (1909–59) WAS THE MOST BRILLIANTLY GIFTED IMPROVISER TO EMERGE BETWEEN ARMSTRONG AND HAWKINS IN THE TWENTIES, AND CHARLIE PARKER IN THE FORTIES. INDEED, SOME WOULD SAY YOUNG WAS THE MOST INSPIRED OF ALL SOLOISTS.

To an extraordinary extent Young had the urge—fundamental to those who play new-minted music every night of their life—to do things differently. He even spoke an impenetrable, self-invented dialect of hip slang. Everyone else held their saxophone upright in front of them, so Young held his sideways like a flute. In the Forties, decades before flower power, he grew his hair long. And the way he played his saxophone was like nothing that had ever been heard before. First of all, there was the question of tone. In the Thirties, all tenor players aimed for Coleman Hawkins's forceful, dark tone. Young's sound was light, wry, lemony—to a naive ear, he might seem to be using a different instrument.

Then there was what he played. Hawkins's style was built around surging harmonic runs; Young sketched oblique melodic lines across the bars. There were no unusual harmonies in what he played. His art lay in playing the ordinary in an extraordinary way, putting the note you least expected in the most

surprising place. He would finger the same note in different ways to change the density of the sound, lag behind the beat, then suddenly catch up with it, use a dozen subtleties to produce music which, as Billie Holiday put it, just flips you out of your seat with surprise.

By all accounts, he formed his style early. His father was a band-leader, and everyone played in the family band. Young spent the early Thirties touring the south-western states with various bands, including one led by the aged King Oliver, and finally ended up in Kansas City. There were no recording studios in that area, however, and he did not record until he travelled West with the Basie band. But in Chicago in 1936, en route for New New York, a small group including Young made a couple of sides—'Lady Be Good' and 'Shoe Shine Swing'—so fresh and buoyant that even Lester could never better them.

For the next 5 years he record-ed extensively with Basie and Billie Holiday, and his music continued to be light-hearted and very inventive.

Unlike Armstrong or Hawkins, who rose powerfully above a large ensemble, Young seems to play tag with the rest of the band, as on the brilliant 'Lester Leaps In' (1939). He could play 2- and 4-bar breaks—like the series at the end of 'Taxi War

Lester Young—president of tenor saxophonists.

Dance' (1940)—so epigramatical-ly perfect they make you feel like laughing out loud. But on the many sides he made with the singer Billie Holiday, in the late Thirties, another side of Young appears. These are performances of the greatest possible intimacy and tenderness.

Then he left Basie, and there is a hiatus in the

recordings; when they start again his sound was heavier, the effect sadder. This change has often been associated with his period in the army, and especially the 16 months he spent in an army detention barracks in 1945–6 (as a punishment for smok-

ing marijuana). But in fact, the alteration had set in even before that awful experience. The truth was that Young was too gentle a soul for the hurly-burly of life; he was a very sensitive man, as his follower Stan Getz remarked, a poet. As he grew older, he grew sadder and drank deeper. He may also have suffered from a syphilitic infection.

His later playing is quite different from the early style— slow, melancholy and sometimes intense-ly moving. Occasionally he was simply too drunk to play well. But almost to the end, there were days when he performed with extraordi-nary emotional truthfulness and beauty, as he did on the sessions from 1956 he made with Teddy Wilson. As Dave Gelly has written, his playing remained "a window on his soul". Towards the end, he would spend long periods in hotels, drinking, listening to records and staring out of the window. After a final trip to Paris—Lester was one of the main models for the central character in Tavernier's film *Round Midnight*—he died at the age of 49.

jazz classics

LOUIS ARMSTRONG

THE HOT FIVES AND SEVENS
Okeh, 1925–8

I N THE OLD DAYS WE USED TO SAY THAT THE RECORD-INGS THAT LOUIS ARMSTRONG MADE IN CHICAGO BETWEEN 1925 and 1928 were quite simply the finest jazz records ever made. These days we're not quite so downright as that, but after six and a half decades these old sides remain a touchstone for what jazz can achieve. Why are they so special? They are certainly not flawless. Armstrong hits a real flub now and again and the earlier *Hot Fives* was hampered by an inadequate rhythm section consisting only of banjo and Lil Armstrong's pedestrian piano (the sides from 1928 with Earl Hines on piano are much better). But tower-ing over the whole series, reducing all faults to unimportance, is the astonishing oratory of Armstrong's trumpet. He took the art of New Orleans men like his mentor King Oliver and raised it to an alto-gether higher artistic power. One can hear him on the *Hot Five* series bursting through the New Orleans convention step by step, inventing the art of the independent jazz soloist. It is hard to choose favourites. The stop time choruses on 'Cornet Chop Suey' and 'Potato Head Blues' fizz with invention and exhilaration. But the most extraordinary set piece is the cadenza to 'West End Blues', a clarion opening as impeccable as anything to be found in Bach.

The same side exemplifies Armstrong's ability to construct a whole performance as a coherent, ordered whole. Armstrong's playing on these sides is filled with a triumphant, life-enhancing strength that places it among the finest music of the century. One of Woody Allen's characters loses his sense of the meaning of life, and finds it again in Armstrong's 'Willie The Weeper'. There aren't many better places.

COUNT BASIE

THE ORIGINAL AMERICAN DECCA RECORDINGS

Decca, 1937–9

THIS IS NOT A CASE FOR MODERATION. EXCEPT FOR A FEW ROUGH EDGES AT THE VERY BEGINNING, AND THE ODD

corny lyric ('Stop Beatin' Around The Mulberry Bush'), the early Basie band was nothing short of perfection. When it arrived in New York in 1937, it carried with it the best of the Kansas City music that had been maturing for a decade. The sound was South-Western, laid back, pared down, blues-based.

No rhythm section has ever been more swinging. No roster of soloists has ever been more inspired—Benny Morton and Dicky Wells among the trombonists, Buck Clayton and Harry Edison in the trumpet section, and the original Texan tenor Herschel Evans among the reeds—while in the other tenor saxophonist, Lester Young, Basie had a supreme jazz improviser at the height of his powers. Time and again, Young comes up with a break or a chorus so imaginative that you could listen to it for ever and it would still sound fresh. His best solos here—on, for example, 'Jumpin' at the Woodside', 'Shorty George', 'Time Out' and 'Doggin' Around'—are brilliant as jazz improvisation ever gets.

Many band vocalists of the day were atrocious, but the spherical Jimmy Rushing (known as "Mr Five-by-Five—five feet high and five feet wide") sang the blues with as much breezy impetus as any of Basie's horn players. Above all, the whole ensemble had a roaring vitality which makes you want to stand up and cheer.

These recordings were the product of a famously iniquitous contract, in which Basie agreed to make 12 sides a year for an annual fee of $750—and no royalties. When the Count moved to Columbia in 1938, he got a better deal, but the band sounded much dimmer.

ORNETTE COLEMAN

THE SHAPE OF JAZZ TO COME

Atlantic, 1959–60

ORNETTE COLEMAN'S EARLY ALBUMS WERE GIVEN APOCALYPTIC, BRAVE NEW WORLD TITLES—CHANGE OF THE

Century, *Tomorrow Is The Question*, and this, *The Shape Of Jazz To Come*—which haven't entirely been borne out by events. Certainly Coleman's ideas did have an important influence on the free jazz movement. But in important respects you have to be Ornette Coleman to play like Ornette Coleman.

Like Miles Davis, Coleman can evoke certain musical moods that no one else can; like Davis he has not changed greatly himself, but been skilful in changing the backgrounds against which his playing is heard. There is not much doubt, however, that the best of all Coleman groups were the ones with which he played in his early years in New York. The first two Coleman albums were marred by musicians unattuned to the master's thought. But the little band he had in 1959–61—with his acolyte Don Cherry on trumpet, Jimmy Garrison or Charlie Haden on bass, Ed Blackwell or Billy Higgins on drums—was just right. The rhythm was loose and springy and Coleman's improvisations were utterly fresh.

A choice from his first three Atlantic albums is a trifle arbitrary, but on balance *The Shape Of Jazz To Come* wins because it has the best tunes. One of Coleman's most engaging traits is an ability to write memorable melodies. Coleman's compositions break the rules, but stay in the mind. They are rooted in the blues and gospel tradition.

This album has the spry 'Congeniality' (inspired by a preacher) and 'Lonely Woman', one of the few Coleman compositions to become a sort of standard, and a prime example of the mood of bleak sadness which he can express as no one else in jazz has ever been able to.

JOHN COLTRANE

GIANT STEPS
Atlantic, 1959

J OHN COLTRANE WAS A MUSICIAN WITH SUCH AN URGE TO MOVE ONWARDS TOWARDS AN UNREACHABLE goal of musical perfection that he scarcely stayed still for long. Almost any document of his playing is a snapshot of a figure in motion. But *Giant Steps* represents something like a moment of mature mastery, free of the strains of the quest or unsatisfactory experiment.

This is a record which wraps up Coltrane's first period, in which he was playing an advanced and complicated form of bebop. This was the era in which he came to stardom as a member of Miles Davis's Quintet, then graduated as a sideman of Thelonious Monk. His goal at this stage was to play everything, all the permutations of each chord—which led to solos of great length—and an effect of cramming of notes, dubbed Coltrane's "sheets of sound".

This aim was difficult enough, but by the time he made *Giant Steps*, he had attained it—which perhaps explains the easy air of this date. *Giant Steps* is a very happy record—not an emotion much associated with Coltrane generally. It bounds along, bursting with energy, Coltrane's tenor seeming to shout with triumph on the title track and 'Mr PC' (named for the bass player Paul Chambers). On the dizzily fast 'Countdown' he is like a man running an Olympic 100 metres and winning in style.

Except on 'Naima'—a tender ballad named for Coltrane's wife—Tommy Flanagan was the pianist on this date, giving him the distinction of having played both on Sonny Rollins's and John Coltrane's finest recordings.

If not Coltrane's greatest album, this is certainly his most likeable one—a record to convince those who cannot take his later modal and free phases that he was indeed a great jazz musician.

MILES DAVIS
KIND OF BLUE
CBS, 1959

THE PROBLEM FACING JAZZ IN THE LATE FIFTIES WAS HOW TO MOVE BEYOND BEBOP. TWENTY YEARS ON, THE HAR-monic freedoms of the Fifties had become constricting—a cage of chords, on which some soloists worked like hamsters on a treadmill.

The answer that Miles Davis toyed with was modality, a solution first proposed by George Russell. Instead of improvising on chords, the soloist would work from a scale or set of scales—so, by freezing harmonic movement, melody could become free and a given idea last as long as the player wished. Davis had already experimented with the notion on his previous album, *Miles Ahead* (1958), made with the same band with John Coltrane on tenor, Cannonball Adderley on alto and the pianist Bill Evans.

This time he threw this astonishing roster of stars in at the deep end. No one had seen the music before the session, indeed Miles had only worked it out hours before. The result, as Evans recalled, was "something close to spontaneity"—and also music with an intensely expressive, sustained mood.

Davis was always master of a certain kind of melodic playing: brooding, introverted, angry. But he never played before or since with quite the same piercing melancholy as on 'Blue In Green'. Or for that matter with the concise, brilliant invention to be heard on 'So What?' and 'All Blues'. Coltrane and Adderley sustain the mood, but the most compelling musician on the date, Davis aside, is Bill Evans.

Indeed, it has been suggested that Davis was inspired by the musical personality of his pianist. But one of Davis's greatest gifts was finding exactly the right context—the right colleagues—for his own playing. He never succeeded better than the day they made *Kind Of Blue*.

MILES DAVIS
BIRTH OF THE COOL
Capitol, 1949-50

THIS BAND THAT DAVIS LED IN 1948-9 WAS SO FAR AHEAD OF ITS TIME THAT IT SCARCE-LY PERFORMED IN PUBLIC-

it once had a 2-week run at a New York club. Its music, however, set the jazz agenda for years to come. The lightweight, nine-piece ensemble represented a radical rethinking of the big band format, one that still sounds fresh today. The most brilliant of the new generation of arrangers—Gerry Mulligan, Gil Evans, John Lewis—contributed charts; the soloists unveiled a new conception of modernism in jazz, less fiery and more melodic than the first wave of bebop. The scoring, instead of following the time-honoured division into brass and reeds, created a new mellow blend which incorporated a tuba and a french horn.

Davis comes across as a genuine leader but Gil Evans was in some ways the guru of the group—certainly his scores 'Moon Dreams' and 'Boplicity' are the most radical and individual (the eery 'Moon Dreams', with its glacial textures, comes close to a definition of "cool"). In fact, almost all the main contributors to the band were members of the coterie who used to meet in Gil Evans's flat on 55th Street, an underground jazz cell where many of the musical developments of the next decade were hatched. In that respect, the tag "birth of the cool" attached to the Davis Nonet is perfectly accurate. But the music is not just a historical landmark; it still delights the ear. In 12 tracks, the only flaw is a vocal performance by Kenny Hagood, a singer with a voice like melted toffee. Otherwise, it's impeccable.

DUKE ELLINGTON

THE WEBSTER-BLANTON BAND
Victor, 1940-2

H IS BAND WAS AT ONCE DUKE ELLINGTON'S GREAT-EST TOOL, HIS GREATEST PLEASURE AND HIS GREATEST CREATION. By general consent, that band reached its peak in the early Forties. At that stage, the musicians with whom he had been working since the late Twenties were as well co-ordinated as a brilliant theatrical company under a great director. But in the late Thirties, new additions to the band raised the whole ensemble to a new height: Ben Webster, a tenor saxophonist who added a new sensuality and masculine force to the band, and the short-lived Jimmy Blanton, the virtual inventor of modern bass-playing.

The masterpieces came very rapidly. If one had to chose just one, it would perhaps be the intensely dramatic 'Ko Ko', with its craggy scoring and plunger-muted trombone from Tricky Sam Nanton so plaintive as to be almost human. But there are dozens almost as good. 'Concerto For Cootie' is a perfectly crafted show-case for the trumpeter Cootie Williams, a master of the plunger-mute and capable of producing a bizarre and wonderful gamut of timbres. 'Warm Valley' and 'Blue Goose' are languorous pieces built around the incomparably mellifluous alto saxophone of Johnny

Hodges. The stop-and-start 'Harlem Air Shaft' is the ideal example of jazz programme music, illustrating all the noises you hear coming up the centre of a New York tenement. They go on and on. Paradoxically, the biggest hit of the lot—'Take The A Train', later Ellington's theme—was not composed by Duke at all, but by another new recruit to the band, arranger/composer Billy Strayhorn.

BILL EVANS
THE VILLAGE VANGUARD SESSIONS
Riverside, 1961

EVANS WAS AS NOTABLE AN INNOVATOR AS ANY IN JAZZ DURING THE LATE FIFTIES AND EARLY SIXTIES. IN ADDITION TO THE colouring classical piano music, which he introduced, and his contribution to modal jazz, he also helped to rethink the jazz group. The

the earliest days can be seen as a process of emancipation. By the late Fifties, the more advanced percussionists were virtually duetting with the soloist—as Philly Joe Jones does to spectacular effect on Bill Evans's first great date. Last to be freed were the bass players. But Evans and his bassist Scott LaFaro had felt their way towards a delicate symbiosis in which Evans was an almost equal partner (Paul Motian, the drummer, played a more subdued role). It took time to do this; the trick is a difficult one. Many who tried to repeat it produced only garrulous tedium—increased freedom is a mixed blessing.

But by June 1961, when these live recordings were made, Evans and LaFaro had reached an extraordinary point of empathy, particularly evident on slow pieces like Evans's own 'Waltz For Debbie'. LaFaro was one of those perfect musical partners that musicians occasionally find—like Jimmy Blanton had been for Ellington. Ten days after these sessions were made, LaFaro was killed in a car accident, aged 25.

ELLA FITZGERALD
THE GERSHWIN SONGBOOK
Verve, 1959

WHEN SHE WAS AT HER VOCAL PEAK, BETWEEN THE MID FORTIES AND THE LATE FIFTIES, ELLA FITZGERALD NEVER REALLY sounded much worse than splendid. That incredibly smooth, creamy voice is a rare musical pleasure in itself, let alone what she did with it. The choice of a single peak amid this mountain range of jazz singing must depend on factors other than pure vocal beauty.

Some composers suit some singers. Ella's gloriously straightforward approach is not quite right for Cole Porter, for example, despite the perennial popularity of her *Cole Porter Songbook*; the worldly sophistication of *Mabel Mercer* is better. Nor is she an ideal interpreter of Rogers and Hart—for that a touch of emotional masochism is required, a

123

smidgeon of sensuality, which Ella does not possess.

But Ella and the Gershwin brothers go together just perfectly. She has a fresh American apple-pie-and-cream quality which combines perfectly with both Ira's words and George's music. Some connoisseurs would say that the very finest Ella of all is to be found among the recordings of Gershwin songs she made in the early Fifties accompanied only by the pianist Ellis Larkins (at present unavailable on CD). But the *Songbook* she recorded later for Norman Granz's Verve label in 1959 is more monumental—amounting to some 53 songs—and in its way just as splendid. Nelson Riddle's arrangements fall mid-way between jazz and Broadway show music—which for the combination of Ella and Gershwin is reasonable enough. Time and time again—on 'Isn't It A Pity', 'I've Got A Crush On You' and 'I've Got Rhythm', for example—she comes up with interpretations which it is hard to imagine either different or better—a high compliment in singing of any kind.

COLEMAN HAWKINS

BODY AND SOUL
Victor, 1939

N O JAZZ SOLOIST STAYED ON TOP FORM FOR AS LONG AS HAWKINS. HE WAS AMONG THE LEADING TENOR SAXOPHONISTS IN jazz—if not actually number one—from the mid Twenties to the early Sixties. But among all his huge recorded output, one short track stands apart: the 3-minute version of 'Body And Soul' which he made on October 11, 1939, both his masterpiece and one of the great achievements of jazz.

In one way it came about casually, in another it was something he had been working up to for his whole musical life. Hawkins's big contribution to jazz—apart from finding a solo voice for the tenor saxophone—was the rhapsodic embellishment of ballads. Indeed, you could almost say that the jazz ballad—now nearly as central to jazz as blues—was Hawkins's invention,

first unveiled in 1929. But a decade later he was at a crisis in his career.

Hawkins had spent the mid and late Thirties in Europe, and in America an assumption had grown up that, although he was an old master certainly, he was perhaps also a bit old hat. He needed to reassert his authority, and he did so, partly by recording 'Body And Soul'.

But the tune was not intended to be anything special; it was something he used to toss off a few choruses of at the end of a performance. He recorded it at the end of a date which produced several inferior sides, but it hit the jackpot both with the public and with musicians. 'Body And Soul's harmonic adventurousness made a big impression on the bebop generation. Hawkins always affected not to see what all the fuss was about, claiming he had played as well live on hundreds of occasions. But 'Body And Soul' is special—utterly spontaneous, unfolding from phrase to phrase, yet structurally perfect. As someone said, it's as beautiful as a flower, enduring as a tombstone—the essence of jazz.

BILLIE HOLIDAY

THE SMALL GROUP SIDES
Columbia, 1935–40

B ILLIE'S CAREER, ROUGHLY SPEAKING, CAME IN THREE PARTS. IN THE FORTIES SHE WAS AT HER VOCAL PEAK, BUT THE SETtings in which she sang were sometimes schmalzy. During her last decade her voice was going—on a bad day she croaked like a raven—but her powers as an interpreter of lyrics were at their height. On balance, her best work came early on, in her first period.

From 1935–41 she made numerous records either with Teddy Wilson and his Orchestra or under her own name. They were intended as cover versions of current tin-pan alley tunes, to be sold cheaply and played in the primeval jukeboxes of the day.

Given the nature of the songs and their market, it's nigh on miraculous

that a number of them turned out as jazz masterpieces. Some of the material is pretty dire, but Billie makes even the worst sound good. She had only to drag that indescribable voice across the words of a lyric for all manner of nuances of feeling to emerge. Despite her somewhat lugubrious reputation, by

no means all of these were sad, and she scarcely ever sang the blues. Sides like 'When You're Smiling' and 'No Regrets' are positively ebullient, with Billie showing herself the equal of the most accomplished jazz musicians of her generation.

Best of all are those from 1937–8 where she is accompanied by Basie musicians, includ-

ing the tenor saxophonist Lester Young. These—for example 'I Can't Get Started', 'Sailboat In The Moonlight', 'Easy Living', 'Me, Myself, I'—document an almost uncannily close musical relationship. Young's saxophone sounds like an echo of Billie's voice. There is no more intimate jazz on record.

THE MODERN JAZZ QUARTET

LAST CONCERT
Atlantic, 1974

A LL KINDS OF INGREDIENTS GO TO MAKE A TRULY GREAT JAZZ PERFORMANCE: THE MUSICIANS AND THEIR MUTUAL compatibility; and, of course, the choice of music that they play. But there is also the question of the occasion. The same performers can play the same piece one night and for some reason—mood, audience, indigestion—nothing much happens. Next day, it's a masterpiece.

Few jazz recordings manage this better than the *Last Concert*. When they made it, the MJQ had existed for over 20 years. For 19, the line-up had been exactly the same—John Lewis on piano, Milt Jackson on vibes, Percy Heath on bass and Connie Kay on drums.

The compositions they played for their farewell concert in

CHARLES MINGUS

THE BLACK SAINT AND THE SINNER LADY
Impulse!, 1963

I T IS TYPICAL OF THE TEMPES-TUOUSLY EMOTIONAL BASSIST, BANDLEADER AND COMPOSER CHARLES MINGUS THAT IT IS hard to select the ideal album to represent his music. Many of his most satisfactory moments as a composer, and his most passionately eloquent bass solos, come scattered among the albums of the late Fifties and early Sixties.

But on balance *The Black Saint And The Sinner Lady* is his finest work. It contains a great deal—though not quite all—of this turbulent man, even to the presentation. The sleevenotes boast an angry outburst by Mingus against not only critics but also one of the musicans on the date. This is followed by another contri-

bution by Mingus's psychiatrist. And to top it off, Mingus—who had taken against the word jazz—forced Impulse Records to classify the result as "Ethnic Folk-Dance Music".

Of course, it is jazz—but jazz created by a sensibility which yearned for the longer forms of classical music (Mingus had trained as a classical cellist). The whole album, in six parts lasting nearly 40 minutes, is one coherent whole. All in all, Mingus here produced the best lengthy, integrated composition jazz has yet achieved.

In this area, Mingus's predecessor—and idol—was Duke Ellington and there are strong Ellingtonian echoes in the voicings, particularly the plunger-muted trombone of Quentin Jackson, a quintessential Ellingtonian sound. But the restless changes of metre and tempo, the swings of mood from gentle romanticism to dissonant sourness and raging chaos are all pure Mingus. The bass player planned an even more ambitious work—*Epitaph*, recorded after his death—but *The Black Saint* is his true monument.

November 1974 were all pieces they had performed innumerable times before. In, effect, this was a programme of greatest hits—John Lewis's 'Django', 'Blues In A Minor', 'The Golden Strike' and so forth. But on this final occasion, for whatever reason, they came up with something special, an extra dimension of intensity and engagement that can be felt even in the orderly lucidity of John Lewis's piano solos. Jackson, always a preacher, is positively fiery on the vibraharp; Percy Heath comes up with an extraordinarily passionate bass improvisation on 'Confirmation'. As Lewis said afterwards, "We all knew that this was it. The end. Either play now, or forget it."

The result was a sort of boiled down compendium of everything that this remarkable group had achieved in the previous two decades. They were not to know, of course, that 19 years later still they would be back together again, playing on a fairly regular basis. But they never sounded better than they did that night at Avery Fisher Hall.

THELONIOUS MONK

THE BLUE NOTE SESSIONS

Blue Note, 1947–52

ESSENTIALLY MONK'S MUSIC WAS FULLY FORMED BY THE TIME HE STARTED TO RECORD FOR BLUE NOTE IN 1947. HE ADDED a few more items to his small corpus of utterly unique compositions in the later Fifties and Sixties, but almost all the most celebrated pieces—'Round Midnight', 'In Walked Bud', 'Straight No Chaser'—were in place early on. Monk's music—beautiful and indispensable as the world of jazz now finds it—took a lot of digesting. It is not so much that the ingredients are novel as that they are put together in such a personal way.

The Blue Note Monk sides are as polished, as perfect, and as completely the expression of a highly individual musical mind as Jelly Roll Morton's Red Hot Peppers sessions in 1926. Each piece is different, each the product of a musical idea or combination of musical ideas reduced to its most intense form. Even the few pieces by other composers which he was in the habit of playing—'April In Paris', for example—have been taken apart and reassembled according to Monk's own principles, to emerge, as Peter Clayton put it, as "cubist portraits of themselves".

To counterbalance the spareness of his own playing, Monk needed relatively garrulous partners. He was not good with Miles Davis, but Milt Jackson, the vibes player who collaborates with Monk on most of the best of these sides, had just the right kind of rolling oratory to fill in over the pianist's acid chords.

Monk is all here on these sides, but it took the rest of us a long time to catch up with him. Someone once asked him why he continued to perform and record the same restricted range of compositions. "I'm going to keep playing them", he replied, "until people start hearing them." Eventually we did.

JELLY ROLL MORTON

THE RED HOT PEPPERS SIDES
Victor, 1926

MORTON WAS REALLY NEI-THER RAGTIME NOR JAZZ BUT WHOLLY INDIVIDUAL—"AS SUBTLY AND INDEFINABLY Mortonian", a critic once wrote, "as Mozart is Mozartian". Jelly was a magnificent solo pianist, but his very finest achievement is to be found on the sessions he made with a band he called the Red Hot Peppers in Chicago in 1926. On these sides Morton produces his own version of the music of his native New Orleans. King Oliver presents the tradition straight, with Morton it is refracted through the sensibility of a fastidious—albeit perhaps unconscious—artist.

Every detail of these sides has been carefully thought out and painstakingly refined. Instead of simply consisting of a theme and impro-

visation, *The Red Hot Peppers Sides* are an intricate succession of different devices. There are scored ensemble passages, solos, stop-time passages, and a profusion of breaks (Jelly later confided that in his view the prop-er use of breaks was one of the keys to the art of jazz). Unusual things occur, like the passage for trumpet, clarinet and trombone without rhythm support which begins 'The Chant'. Jelly was very fond of odd-ball combinations—clarinet with banjo accompaniment, for example. A couple of sides—'Sidewalk Blues' and 'Deadman Blues'—begin with little spoken dramas.

It could all have easily turned out contrived and bitty. But each piece somehow comes together into a unified whole, and a whole that is imbued with the indefinable happy-sad spirit of Jelly Roll. *The Peppers Sides* have the essential spontaneity of jazz. Others—Ellington, Mingus, Monk—have also succeeded in squaring the circle of composing jazz without losing its spirit. But Jelly did it first, and no one has ever really bettered him.

KING OLIVER

THE CREOLE JAZZ BAND SIDES
Various, 1923–4

ALTHOUGH A WHITE NEW ORLEANS BAND MADE THE FIRST JAZZ RECORDS IN 1917, THE RECORDINGS KING OLIVER'S Creole Jazz Band made in Chicago in 1923 are the classic examples of the style, the final flower of two decades' evolution. The music is constantly mobile and full of vari-ety. Unlike much of what passed for jazz in the Twenties, it is never rau-cous or forced. It flows sweetly, almost gently.

Oliver liked to have his band play so softly sometimes you could hear the shuffle of the dancers' feet, and always, as one of his musicians put it, "for the comfort of the people". There is probably no better exam-ple of the New Orleans ensemble style than the Creole Jazz Band's 'Snake Rag'.

Oliver was also a great leader, but he was also an important performer in his own right, subtle and driving. His climactic solo on 'Dippermouth Blues', recorded in 1923, is still elating nearly 70 years after it was first played. His deep blue, muted sound still punches out of these ancient records; there is little in later jazz more dynamic than his breaks on 'Sobbin' Blues'. He had an ability which, though hard to define, is essential in jazz: Oliver swung. Most of his colleagues were just as distinguished; Louis Armstrong arguably was already even more so. Much of the time Armstrong played a second part to Oliver—they often played duets together—but once or twice, as on 'Tears And Riverside Blues', he rings out on his own. It is the sound, as Humphrey Lyttelton put it, of genius emerging; Johnny Dodds plays admirable New Orleans clarinet, the trombonist Honore Dutrey less distinguished. But Lilian Hardin (later Mrs Armstrong) tends to plod along on piano; entirely swinging rhythm sections still lay in the future.

CHARLIE PARKER
Ko Ko
Savoy, 1945

IF THERE HAD NOT BEEN A MUSICIANS' UNION BAN ON RECORDING FROM LATE 1942 TO 1944, WE WOULD BE BETTER informed about the evolution of bebop. As it is, there are a few sides in which Parker and Gillespie work with transitional bands—a bop front line, swing rhythm section. Then on November 26, 1945, bang, the first full bebop record session—a landmark as important as any in the history of jazz.

In some ways Charlie Parker managed to say more or less all he had to say on this first session under his own name, and a great deal of it on one piece: 'Ko Ko' (not to be confused with the Ellington composition of the same name). Like Hawkins's 'Body And Soul', Parker's 'Ko Ko' had been a long time maturing. He was already breaking up audiences with this chord

sequence—'Ko Ko' is actually based on the harmonies of Ray Noble's 'Cherokee'—while still working with Jay McShann in 1942. Three years on it had become the perfect vehicle for everything he wanted to do with up-tempo jazz.

'Ko Ko' is a marvel; for its time it was unbelievably fast (indeed, it is still very hard to play at this rate). But no matter how fast the pace, Parker's mind worked faster. His solo is an extraordinary cornucopia of ideas, tumbling out one after another, flashing past so rapidly it is hard for the listener to take them in. As a piece of virtuosity and whirlwind musical invention, 'Ko Ko' sets a standard for all time.

Much of the rest of the best of Parker was also recorded for the Savoy label. There is a marvellous blues—'Now's The Time'—from that first 1945 date. But his blues masterpiece is 'Parker's Mood' from a 1948 session with John Lewis on piano. 'Bird Gets The Worm' from 1947 comes close to rivalling 'Ko Ko'—but nothing even Parker played since does quite does.

ART PEPPER

ART PEPPER MEETS THE RHYTHM SECTION
Contemporary, 1957

JAZZ IS A SPONTANEOUS MUSIC, SOMETIMES ASTONISHINGLY SO, A TRUTH OF WHICH THIS ALBUM IS AN OUTSTANDING illustration. The alto saxophonist Art Pepper was a West Coast player; the rest of the band—the rhythm section—worked with the Miles Davis Quintet based in New York.

That, however, was not so much the problem as that Pepper and the rest had not played or rehearsed together before. Worse still, Pepper—who was deeply addicted to various drugs and was in and out of jail at this time—was in an appalling state. Apparently he was actually spinning on his heels during the date.

But strangely, the result was a masterpiece. Pepper was harmonically a post-Parker musician, but he

also had something of poise of the swing master Benny Carter (his affinity with early jazz is brought out by the choice of the dixieland standard 'Jazz Me Blues' for this date). In addition, he had an emotional edge of his own. Perhaps the challenge of meeting this rhythm section helped to bring that out—he talked about overcoming his inhibitions. Or perhaps it was the excellence of the other musicians. In 1957, this trio—with Paul Chambers on bass, Red Garland on piano, and Philly Joe Jones on drums—was *the* rhythm section in jazz. And it's not hard to see why. This was one of most delightful points on the path to complete autonomy—some would say anarchy—that bassist, drummers and pianists enjoyed in the Sixties. Garland was a romantic melodist given to block chording, Chambers kept the time, while Philly Joe—a great drummer—played wild, nervy cross rhythms. In places this session is virtually a duet—intense yet controlled—between Pepper and the whip-lash drumming of Jones. It's terrific.

SONNY ROLLINS

SAXOPHONE COLOSSUS
Prestige, 1956

SONNY ROLLINS—LIKE SEVERAL OF HIS CONTEMPORARIES—REPRESENTED A CLARIFICATION OF THE FIRST GENERATION OF bop. There is a beautifully logical structure in the best of Rollins's Fifties work which is nowhere more evident than in the finest of his early albums, *Saxophone Colossus*.

To Rollins's chagrin, the masterpiece of the session, 'Blue Seven', was subjected to a lengthy analysis in terms of themes and variation by the critic Gunther Schuller, just as if it had been a classical composition. But Schuller had a point. One of the gripping things about this long and gripping track is the clarity with which every part of the performance is related to its predecessor.

On this album Rollins was returning in a way to the principles of the best swing musicians like Louis Armstrong and Lester Young, who always laid great emphasis on "telling a story". (Thelonious Monk, a mentor of Rollins's, also used to ask: "Why don't we use the melody?") In contrast some of the lesser boppers tended just to "run the changes"—go through the chords. Rollins's massive tone might be seen too as a throwback to the days of Webster and Hawkins—except that it entirely omitted the carefully burnished vibrato of those men. Indeed, in contrast Rollins might sound harsh, brusque, disobliging—one critic called his sound "goatlike"—but of course it was beautiful in a newer, different way. In retrospect, he even sounds romantic enough on the ballad 'You Don't Know What Love Is'.

Rollins has done many other things in the years since this session, some very different. But on that day in 1956, with his tenor balanced by the crystalline precision of Roach's drumming and Tommy Flanagan's unflurried piano, he touched a moment of rare perfection.

ART TATUM

THE GROUP MASTERPIECES

Verve, 1954–6

THE VIRTUOSITY OF ART TATUM WAS SO EXTRAORDINARY THAT IT WAS ALMOST AN EMBARRASSMENT TO JAZZ.

Indeed, even in classical terms it was a phenomenon. Vladimir Horovitz, as remarkable a technician as this century has seen, once confessed that, though he could play the same notes as Tatum, he could not maintain the same rhythmic pulse.

Tatum spent most of the early part of his career working either as an isolated soloist or with a trio of bass and guitar. It was not until he was signed up by the impresario Norman Granz late in his short life that the full range and depth of his talent were properly documented. Scholars of Tatum's solo style will want the monumental series of solo performances which Granz took down between 1953 and 1955. But more ordinary mortals will probably find a better introduction to him in the group performances which Granz made at the same time.

The seven sessions brought out different aspects of Tatum the pianist. The trio date with the ex-Basie drummer Jo Jones was notable for straight-ahead, driving swing. When Tatum was paired with Lionel Hampton on vibes and Buddy Rich on drums—two of the very few musicians in jazz who could come close to matching Tatum's technical facility—ebullient effervescence resulted. Performing with the elegant melodist Benny Carter on alto, Tatum the rhapsodist was more to the fore. Even more romantic, and best of all, was the combination of the pianist with the tenor saxophonist Ben Webster. Webster was a player with a huge sound and a stately approach, and he responded to the challenge of playing with Tatum by simply remaining himself. His tenor sails majestically along on the tide of piano to incomparably sumptuous effect.

SIDNEY BECHET
Sidney Bechet,
1932–43: The
Bluebird Sessions
1932–43
UK: BLUEBIRD ND 90317 5CD
The Chronological
Sidney Bechet,
1937–1938 *1937–8*
UK: CLASSICS 593 CD
The Victor Sessions:
The Master Takes
1932–43
US: BLUEBIRD 2402

BIX BEIDERBECKE
1927
UK: JSP CDR 316
Bix Beiderbecke Vol
1: Singin' The Blues
1927
UK: CBS VCK-45450
Bix Beiderbecke Vol
II: At The Jazz Band
Ball *1927–8*
UK: CBS VCK 46175
Bix Lives! *1927–30*
US: BLUEBIRD ND 85845

RUBY BRAFF
Bravura Eloquence
1988
US: CONCORD JAZZ CCD-4423
Ruby Braff And His
New England
Songhounds Vol 1
1991
US: CONCORD JAZZ CCD-4423
Ruby Braff And His
New England
Songhounds Vol 2
1991

A Night at Birdland
Vol 1 *1954*
UK: CONCORD JAZZ CCD-4504
Ruby Braff Salutes
Rodgers And Hart
1974
US: CONCORD JAZZ CCD-4504

BENNY CARTER
3, 4, 5 The Verve
Small Group
Sessions *1950s*
UK: VERVE 849395-2

BETTY CARTER
Betty Carter:
Compact Jazz
1976–87
UK: VERVE 843274-2
Finally *1969*
US: BLUE NOTE B21Y-95333
I Can't Help It
1958–61
US: GRP GRD-114

DOC CHEATHAM
NO CDs CURRENTLY AVAILABLE

A Night at
Birdland Vol 2 *1954*
UK: BLUE NOTE BNZ-9
Art Blakey's Jazz
Messengers With
Thelonious Monk
1957
UK: ATLANTIC 781332
At The Cafe
Bohemia Vol 1 *1955*
US: BLUE NOTE B21Y-46521
At The Cafe
Bohemia Vol 2 *1955*
US: BLUE NOTE B21Y-46522
Free For All *1964*
US: BLUE NOTE BNZ-5
Moanin' *1958*
UK: BLUE NOTE BNZ-4
Mosaic *1961*
UK: BLUE NOTE BNZ-7
The Big Beat *1960*
UK: BLUE NOTE BNZ-2

CLIFFORD BROWN
At Basin Street East
(With Max Roach)
1956
Complete
Recordings Vol 1
1954–6
UK: EMARCY 814648
Brownie: The
Complete Emarcy
Recordings (10 CDs)
1954–6
UK: EMARCY 838 306-2
Clifford Brown Big
Band In Paris
1953
US: ORIGINAL JAZZ CLASSICS
OJCCD-359-2
Study In Brown
(With Max Roach)
1954
UK: POLYGRAM 814646-2

DAVE BRUBECK
Jazz At Oberlin
1953
UK: FANTASY CDRIVM-007
US: ORIGINAL JAZZ CLASSICS
OJCD 046-2
The Dave Brubeck
Octet *1948–9*
US: ORIGINAL JAZZ CLASSICS
OJCD 101-2
Time Out *1959*
UK: CBS 460611-2

All of Me *1940*
US: POLYGRAM 849395-2
US: RCA BLUEBIRD 3000-2
Central City
Sketches *1987*
UK: MUSICMASTERS CIJD-
60126X
Complete
Recordings Vol 1
1932–40
UK: AFFINITY AFS-1022-3
Devil's Holiday *1934*
UK: JSP JSPCD-331
Further Definitions
1961
UK: MCA MCAD-5651
US: MCA MCAD-5651
Harlem Renaissance
1992
US: MUSICMASTERS 65085
Jazz Giant
1957–8
US: ORIGINAL JAZZ CLASSICS
OJC 167
Swinging the
Twenties *1958*
US: ORIGINAL JAZZ CLASSICS
OJC 167

CHARLIE CHRISTIAN
Charlie Christian
And Lester Young
1939–40
UK: ARCHIVES OF JAZZ
3801422
Charlie Christian
And Lester Young
Together *1940*
UK: ARCHIVES OF JAZZ
3801062
Charlie Christian
And The Benny
Goodman Sextet
Live *1939–41*
UK: ARCHIVES OF JAZZ
3801232
Genius of the
Electric Guitar
1939–41
UK: CBS JAZZ MASTERPIECES
460612-2
Solo Flight *1939–41*
US: VINTAGE JAZZ 1021

BUCK CLAYTON
Jam Sessions fr_
the Vault *195_

UK: CBS JAZZ MASTERS
463336-2

NAT KING COLE
After Midnight 1956
UK: CAPITOL CDEMS-1103
Anatomy of a Jam Session 1945
US: BLACK LION 760137
The Trio Recordings Vol 1 1941
US: LASERLIGHT 15746
The Trio Recordings Vol 2 1942
US: LASERLIGHT 15747
The Trio Recordings Vol 3 1942–3
US: LASERLIGHT 15748
The Trio Recordings Vol 4 1944–5
US: LASERLIGHT 15749
The Trio Recordings Vol 5 1945
US: LASERLIGHT 15750

ORNETTE COLEMAN
At The Golden Circle, Stockholm Vol 1 1965
UK: BLUE NOTE BNZ-180
US: BLUE NOTE B21Y-84224
At The Golden Circle, Stockholm Vol 2 1965
US: BLUE NOTE B21Y-84225
Change Of The Century 1959
US: ATLANTIC 81341-2
Something Else! 1958
US: ORIGINAL JAZZ CLASSICS OJCC-163-2
The Shape of Jazz

To Come 1960
UK: ATLANTIC 781339-2
Tomorrow Is The Question 1959
US: ORIGINAL JAZZ CLASSICS OJCCD-342-2

JOHN COLTRANE
A Love Supreme 1965
UK: IMPULSE MCAD-5660
US: MCA MCAD-5660
Africa Brass Vols I and 2 1961
UK: MCA IMPULSE MCAD 42001
US: MCA MCAD 42001
Ballads 1962
UK: IMPULSE MCAD 5885
US: MCA MCAD 5885
Blue Train 1957
UK: BLUE NOTE BNZ-21
Coltrane 1962
UK: IMPULSE MCAD 5883
US: MCA MCAD 5883
Coltrane And Ellington 1962
UK: IMPULSE MCAD 39103
US: MCA MCAD 39103
Giant Steps 1959
UK: ATLANTIC 781337-2
Live at the Village Vanguard 1961
UK: MCA MCAD 39136
US: MCA MCAD 39136
Lush Life 1957–8
UK: FANTASY VDJ-1544
US: PRESTIGE OJCCD-131-2
My Favourite Things 1960
US: ATLANTIC 781346-2
Soultrane 1958
UK: PRESTIGE CDRIVM-003
US: PRESTIGE OJCCD-021-2
Traneing In 1957

UK: PRESTIGE CDRIVM-004 OJCCD 189-2
US: ORIGINAL JAZZ CLASSICS CL OJCCD-189-2

EDDIE CONDON
Ballin' The Jack 1940–3
US:COMMODORE 7016
Dixieland Jam 1957
US: COLUMBIA 45145
Live at the New School (with Wellstood, Davern, Davison and Krupa) 1972
US: CHIAROSCURO 110
Live at Town Hall–Legendary Jam 1944
US: JASS 634

CHICK COREA
Piano Improvisations Vol 1 1971
UK: ECM 811979-2
US: ECM 811979-2
Piano Improvisations Vol 2 1971
UK: ECM 829190-2
US: ECM 829190-2

BOB CROSBY
Bob Crosby 1937–8
UK: BBC BBCCD-668
South Rampart Street Parade 1936–42
UK: GRP-16152
US: GRP GRD-615

TADD DAMERON
Fontainebleau 1956
US: ORIGINAL JAZZ CLASSICS CL OJCCD-05-2
The Magic Touch 1962
US: ORIGINAL JAZZ CLASSICS CL OJCCD-143-2

KENNY DAVERN
Dick Wellstood And His Famous Orchestra Featuring Kenny Davern 1973–82
US: CHIAROSCURO 129
Live At The New School (With Wellstood, Condon, Krupa And Davison) 1972
US: CHIAROSCURO 110
Soprano Summit In Concert 1976
UK: CONCORD JAZZ CCD 4029
US: CONCORD JAZZ CCD 4029
Soprano Summit Live At Concord 1977
UK: CONCORD JAZZ CCD 4052
US: CONCORD JAZZ CCD 4052
Summit Reunion 1990
US: CHIAROSCURO CR(D) 311

EDDIE "LOCKJAW" DAVIS
The Cookbook Vol 1 1958
US: ORIGINAL JAZZ CLASSICS CL OJCD 652-2
The Cookbook Vol 2

1958
US: ORIGINAL JAZZ CLASSICS CL OJCD 653-2

MILES DAVIS
Birth of the Cool 1949–50
US: CAPITOL CDP 792862
Cookin' 1956
US: ORIGINAL JAZZ CLASSICS OJCCD-128-2
Kind of Blue 1959
UK: COLUMBIA CD-62066
US: COLUMBIA 40579
Miles Ahead 1957
UK: COLUMBIA JAZZ MASTERPIECES 460606-2
Miles Davis Vol 1 1952–54
UK: BLUE NOTE BNZ 111
Milestones 1958
UK: COLUMBIA 460827-2
UK:COLUMBIA VCK -40647
Relaxin' 1956
US: ORIGINAL JAZZ CLASSICS OJCCD-190-2
Porgy & Bess 1958
UK:COLUMBIA VCK-40647
Sketches of Spain 1959
UK: COLUMBIA JAZZ MASTERPIECES 460604-2
Walkin' 1954
US: PRESTIGE CDRIVM-004
Workin' 1956
US:PRESTIGE OJCCD-296-2

JOHNNY DODDS
Blue Clarinet Stomp 1926–9
UK: BLUEBIRD ND 82293 CD
UK: RCA 2293-2

Jazz Classics 1926–8
US: BBC BBCGD-603
Johnny Dodds,
1926–40: Part One
1926–40
UK: AFFINITY CD AFS
1023 3CD
South Side Chicago
Jazz 1927–9
US: MCA MCAD 42326

ERIC DOLPHY
At The Five Spot
Vol 1 1960
US: ORIGINAL JAZZ CLASSICS CL
OJCD 133-2
At The Five Spot
Vol 2 1960
US: PRESTIGE OJCCD 247-2
Memorial Album
1961
US: ORIGINAL JAZZ CLASSICS
CL OJCD 353-2
Out to Lunch 1964
UK: BLUE NOTE BNZ-23

ROY ELDRIDGE
After You've Gone
1936–46
UK: GRP GRP-10652
Artie Shaw: Blues in
the Night 1941–5
UK: BLUEBIRD ND-90628
US: BLUEBIRD 2432-2
The Nifty Cat 1970
UK: NEW WORLD
NWCD-349.2
US: NEW WORLD
Masterpieces Vol 2
1935

US: PABLO 2405432
Uptown with the
Gene Krupa
Orchestra 1941–9
US: COLUMBIA 45448

DUKE ELLINGTON
...And His Mother
Called Him Bill 1967
US: BLUEBIRD 6287-2
Back To Back 1959
UK: RCA BLUEBIRD ND 86287
Blues In Orbit 1959
UK: COLUMBIA 460823
Braggin' In Brass—
The Immortal 1938
Year 1938
US: PORTRAIT R2K 44395
Duke Ellington and
John Coltrane 1962
UK: MCA MCAD 39103
Duke's Big Four
1973
UK: PABLO 2310721
Early Ellington
1927–34
UK: BLUEBIRD 86852 CD
US: BLUEBIRD 6852-2
Fargo, ND 11/7/40
1940
UK: VINTAGE JAZZ CLASSICS
VJC 873-000
US: VINTAGE JAZZ CLASSICS
1019
Jungle Nights in
Harlem
1927–32
UK: CARRERE 98944
US: RCA 2499
Money Jungle
1962
UK: BLUE NOTE BNZ-29

The Blanton-
Webster Years
1940–2
UK: RCA BLUEBIRD 85659 3
CD
US: BLUEBIRD 5659
The Duke's Men:
Small Groups Vol 1
1934–8
US: COLUMBIA 46861 8 2CD
The Duke's Men:
Small Groups Vol 2
1934–8
UK: COLUMBIA 472994 2CD
The Ellington Suites
1959, 1971, 1972
UK: PABLO OJCCD 446
US: PABLO OJCCD 446
The Far East Suite
1966
UK: RCA BLUEBIRD ND 87640
The Great Ellington
Units 1940–1
UK: RCA BLUEBIRD ND 86751
US: BLUEBIRD 6751-2
The Great Paris
Concert 1963
UK: WEA CD-00-304
This One's For
Blanton 1972
US: PABLO 2310721

1961
US: ORIGINAL JAZZ CLASSICS
OJCCD-140-2
Undercurrent
(With Jim Hall) 1962
UK: BLUE NOTE BNZ167
Waltz For Debbie
1961
UK: RIVERSIDE OJCCD-210-2
US: ORIGINAL JAZZ CLASSICS
OJCCD-210-2

GIL EVANS
Gil Evans And Ten
1957
US: SONY MUSIC 46995
New Bottle, Old
Wine 1960
UK: EMI CZ-50
Out Of The Cool
1960
UK: EMI CZ-51
The Individualism
Of Gil Evans 1963–4
US: POLYGRAM 833804-2

ART FARMER
Meet The Jazztet
1960
US: CHESS CHD-91550
Modern Art 1958
UK: BLUE NOTE B21Y-84459
US: BLUE NOTE B278
Portrait Of Art
Farmer 1958
US: ORIGINAL JAZZ CLASSICS
OJCCD-166-2

ELLA FITZGERALD
75th Birthday
Celebration 1938–55
UK: GRP 26192
Compact Jazz: Ella
Fitzgerald 1957–65
US: POLYGRAM 831367-2
Compact Jazz: Ella
Fitzgerald Live
1956–66
US: POLYGRAM 833294-2
Ella And Louis 1950
UK: POLYGRAM 825373-2
Harold Arlen
Songbook Vol 1
1960–61
UK: POLYGRAM 817527 2CD
Harold Arlen
Songbook Vol 2
1960–1
UK: POLYDOR 817528 2CD
Take Love Easy
(With Joe Pass) 1973
UK: PABLO CD 2310702
The Cole Porter
Songbook Vol 1
1956
UK: VERVE 821989
The Cole Porter
Songbook Vol 2
1956
UK: VERVE 821990
The Duke Ellington
Songbook 1956–7
US: POLYGRAM 837035-2
The Early Years Part
1 1935–8
UK: MCA GRP 26182
The George And Ira
Gershwin Songboo
1959
UK: VERVE 821024-2

The Irving Berlin Songbook Vol 1 *1958*
UK: VERVE 829534
The Jerome Kern Songbook *1963*
UK: VERVE 821669 2CDThe
Johnny Mercer Songbook *1964*
UK: POLYGRAM 821247 2CD
The Rogers And Hart Songbook Vol 1 *1956*
UK: POLYGRAM 821579
The Rogers And Hart Songbook Vol 2 *1956*
UK: POLYGRAM 821580 2 CD

TOMMY FLANAGAN
Ballads And Blues *1978*
UK: ENJA-3031-2
Giant Steps *1982*
US: RHINO 79646-2
Jazz Poet *1989*
UK: TIMELESS CDSJP-301
The Tommy Flanagan Trio *1960*
US: ORIGINAL JAZZ CLASSICS OJCCD-182-2

ERROLL GARNER
Compact Jazz: Erroll Garner *1954-5*
UK: POLYGRAM 830695-2
US: POLYGRAM 830695-2
Jazz Around Midnight *1945-5*
UK: POLYGRAM 846191-2
US: POLYGRAM 846191-2

STAN GETZ
At Storyville *1951*
US: BLUE NOTE B21Y - 94507
Compact Jazz: Stan Getz *1953-7*
UK: POLYGRAM 831368-2
Early Stan *1949-53*
UK: ORIGINAL JAZZ CLASSICS OJCCD 654-2
Focus *1965*
UK: POLYGRAM 821982-2
Jazz Samba *1962*
UK: POLYGRAM 810061-2
Serenity *1987*
UK: EMARCY 838770-2
US: POLYGRAM 838770-2
Spring Is Here *1981*
UK: CONCORD JAZZ CCD 4500
US: CONCORD JAZZ CCD 4500
The Best Of The Verve Years Vol 2 *1951-71*
UK: VERVE 517 330-2
The Dolphin *1981*
UK: CONCORD JAZZ CCD-4158
US: CONCORD JAZZ CCD-4158

DIZZY GILLESPIE
A Portrait of Duke Ellington *1960*
UK: POLYGRAM 817110-2
Compact Jazz (Big Band) *1955-62*
US: POLYGRAM 831393-2
Compact Jazz: Dizzy Gillespie *1954-64*
UK: POLYGRAM 832574-2
Dizzy's Diamonds: The Best of the Verve Years *1954-64*
UK: VERVE 513875-2
US: VERVE 513875-2

Jazz Round Midnight *1954-64*
UK: POLYGRAM 51088-2
Shaw'Nuff *1945-6*
US: MUSICRAFT MVSCD-53
The Bebop Revolution (with other artists) *1940s*
UK: BLUEBIRD ND-82177
US: BLUEBIRD 2177-2

JIMMY GIUFFRE
Jimmy Giuffre 3 *1961*
UK: ECM 849644-2
US: POLYGRAM 849644-2

BENNY GOODMAN
After You've Gone: Original Benny Goodman Trio & Quartet Sessions Vol 1 *1935-7*
UK: BLUEBIRD ND 85631
US: BLUEBIRD 6283-2
BG And Big Tea In NYC *1929-34*
UK: MCA GRP-16092
US: GRP GRD-609
Carnegie Hall Concert Part 1 *1938*
US: GIANTS OF JAZZ CD-53101
Carnegie Hall Concert Part 2 *1938*
US: GIANTS OF JAZZ CD-53102
The Harry James Years Vol 1 *1937-8*
UK: BLUEBIRD 07863 66155 2
Yale Archives Vol 1 *1955-86*
UK: LIMELIGHT 8208022

DEXTER GORDON
A Swingin' Affair *1962*
UK: BLUE NOTE BNZ-31
US: BLUE NOTE B21Y-84133
Best of Dexter Gordon (The Blue Note Years) *1961-2*
US: BLUE NOTE BNZ-275
Dexter Calling *1961*
UK: BLUE NOTE BNZ-36
Doin' Alright *1961*
UK: BLUE NOTE BNZ-113
Getting Around *1965*
UK: BLUE NOTE BNZ-32
Go *1962*
UK: BLUE NOTE BNZ-33
One Flight Up! *1964*
UK: BLUE NOTE BNZ-36
Our Man in Paris *1963*
UK: BLUE NOTE BNZ-34

STEPHANE GRAPPELLI
Compact Jazz: Stephane Grappelli *1971-9*
UK: POLYGRAM 831370-2
Parisian Thoroughfare *1973*
US: BLACK LION 760132
Tivoli Gardens, Copenhagen, Denmark *1979*
UK: PABLO CD-20041
Vintage 1981 *1981*
UK: CONCORD JAZZ CCD4169

BOBBY HACKETT
Coast Concert/Jazz

Ultimate *1955-7*
UK: DORMOUSE INTERNATIONAL DMI CDX 02
Gotham Jazz Scene *1957*
UK: DORMOUSE DMI CDX CDX 03
Live at the Roosevelt Grill *1969*
US: CHIAROSCURO 105

JIM HALL
Jazz Guitar *1957*
UK: BLUE NOTE CZ-68
Live At Village West (With Ron Carter) *1984*
UK: CONCORD JAZZ CCD-4245
US: CONCORD JAZZ CCD-4245
Undercurrent (With Bill Evans) *1962*
UK: BLUE NOTE BNZ-167

SCOTT HAMILTON
Major League *1986*
US: CONCORD JAZZ CCD-4305
Race Point *1991*
UK: CONCORD JAZZ CCD-4492
US: CONCORD JAZZ CCD-4492
Radio City *1990*
UK: CONCORD JAZZ CCD-44428

LIONEL HAMPTON
Flyin' Home *1942-5*
US: MCA MCAD-42349
Hamp And Getz *1955*
UK: POLYGRAM 831672-2
US: POLYGRAM 831672-2
Hot Mallets Vol 1 *1937-9*
UK: BLUEBIRD ND 86458

US: BLUEBIRD 86458
Just Jazz 1947
UK: GNP 655604
US: MCA 42329

Lionel Hampton
1929–40
UK: BBC RPCD-852

**Lionel Hampton:
Compact Jazz**
1954–5
US: POLYGRAM 833287-2

Reunion at Newport
1967
US: BLUEBIRD 07863 66157-2

Tempo And Swing
1939–40
UK: BLUEBIRD 4321-101161-2
US: RCA 66039-2

The Jumpin Jive
1937–9
UK: POLYGRAM 833287-2

**The Tatum Group
Masterpieces
Vols 3, 4, 5**
1955
US: PABLO 240543-4, -5, -6

ROY HARGROVE
The Vibe 1992
UK: NOVUS 631132-2
US: NOVUS 631132-2

COLEMAN HAWKINS
**At Ease With
Coleman Hawkins**
1960
UK: ORIGINAL JAZZ CLASSICS
CL OJCCD-181-2
US: ORIGINAL JAZZ CLASSICS
CL OJCCD-181-2

Body And Soul
1939–56
UK: BLUEBIRD ND 85717-2

**Classic Tenors
(with Lester Young)**
1944
US: DOCTOR JAZZ 38446

Hawk Eyes 1959
US: ORIGINAL JAZZ CLASSICS
OJCD 294-2

**Hollywood
Stampede** 1945
UK: EMI USA C21H-92594
US: CAPITOL C21Y-92596

Soul 1958
OJCD 096

**The Genius of
Coleman Hawkins**
1957
UK: LONDON 8206002

**The High And
Mighty Hawk** 1958
UK: POLYGRAM 8256732

FLETCHER HENDERSON
Hocus Pocus 1933
UK: BLUEBIRD ND-90413
US: BLUEBIRD 9904-2

**Jazz Classics in
Digital Stereo**
1925–8
US: CBS 462401-2

**The Chronological
Fletcher Henderson
Vol 1** 1927
UK: JAZZ CLASSICS-580

**The Chronological
Fletcher Henderson
Vol 2** 1927–31
UK: JAZZ CLASSICS-572

JOE HENDERSON
Inner Urge 1964
UK: BLUE NOTE BNZ 228

**Lee Morgan: The
Sidewinder** 1963
UK: BLUE NOTE BNZ 66

Mode For Joe 1966
US: BLUE NOTE B21Y 84227

Page One 1963
US: BLUE NOTE B21Y 84140

**The Best Of Joe
Henderson** 1963–85
UK: BLUE NOTE CDP 7956272

EARL HINES
Blues in Thirds 1965
US: BLACK LION 760120

Earl Hines
1932–4, 1937
UK: ARCHIVES OF JAZZ
380 1022

**Live at the Village
Vanguard** 1965
UK: CBS 462401-2

Piano Man 1937–42
US: BLUEBIRD ND 86750

**Plays Duke
Ellington**
1971–5
US: NEW WORLD 361

Tour de Force 1972
US: BLACK LION 760140

**Tour de Force
Encore** 1972
US: BLACK LION 760157

JOHNNY HODGES
Everybody knows
1964
UK: IMPULSE GRP 1116-2

Used to be Duke
1954
US: VERVE 849394-2

BILLIE HOLIDAY
**Compact Jazz: Billie
Holiday** 1955–6
UK: POLYGRAM 831371-2

Lady In Autumn
1946–59
US: VERVE 849434-2

**Songs for Distingué
Lovers** 1956
UK: POLYGRAM 8150055-2

**The Complete Decca
Sessions** 1944–50
US: GRP GRD2-601

**The Quintessential
Billie Holiday Vol 4**
1937
UK: COLUMBIA 463333-2

**The Quintessential
Billie Holiday Vol 5**
1937–8
US: COLUMBIA JAZZ
MASTERPIECES 465190
US: COLUMBIA 44423

**The Voice of Jazz:
The Complete
Recordings**
1933–40
UK: AFFINITY CDASE 1019
US: D. COLEMAN HAWKINS

ILLINOIS JACQUET
Black Velvet Band
1947–9
UK: BLUEBIRD ND-86571
US: RCA 6571-2

Blues—That's Me!
1969
US: ORIGINAL JAZZ CLASSICS
CL OJCCD-614-2

**JARRETT KEITH
JARRETT**
Silence 1975
UK: IMPULSE GRP 117-2

Expectations
1971
US: SONY MUSIC 46866

J. J. JOHNSON
**Live at the Cafe
Bohemia** 1957
UK: FRESH SOUNDS FSCD-143

Say When 1964–6
UK: BLUEBIRD ND-86277
UK: BLUEBIRD 6277

The Birdlanders
1954
UK: FRESH SOUNDS FSCD-170

JAMES P. JOHNSON
**Snowy Morning
Blues** 1930–44
US: GRP GRD-604

HANK JONES
Hank Solo Piano
1976
US: ALL ART JAZZ AAJ 11003

Tiptoe Tapdance
1977-8
US: ORIGINAL JAZZ CLASSICS OJCCD-719-2

STAN KENTON
New Concepts of Artistry in Rhythm
1952
UK: EMI CZ 299

LEE KONITZ
I Concentrate On You *1974*
UK: STEEPLECHASE SCS 1018
Subconscious-Lee
1949-50
ORIGINAL JAZZ CLASSICS OJCC 186-2
The Lee Konitz Duets *1967*
US: ORIGINAL JAZZ CLASSICS OJCCD 466-2

JIMMY LUNCEFORD
Rhythm Is Our Business *1934-40*
UK: LIVING ERA AJACD-5091
Stomp It Off *1934-5*
US: MCA GRP-16082
The Chronological Jimmie Lunceford *1939-40*
US: GRP GRD-608

WYNTON MARSALIS
Blue Interlude *1992*
US: SONY MUSIC 48729
The Majesty Of The Blues *1988*
UK: SONY MUSIC 465129-2

JACKIE McLEAN
Let Freedom Ring
1963
UK: BLUE NOTE BNZ-59
New Soil *1959*
UK: BLUE NOTE CDP-784013-2
One Step Beyond *1963*
UK: BLUE NOTE BNZ-60

CARMEN McRAE
No CDs CURRENTLY AVAILABLE

CHARLES MINGUS
Blues and Roots *1959*
UK: ATLANTIC 781336-2
Mingus, Mingus, Mingus, Mingus, Mingus *1963*
UK: MCA IMPULSE MCAD-39119
New Tijuana Moods *1957*
UK: BLUEBIRD ND-85644
US: BLUEBIRD 5644-2
Pithecanthropus Erectus *1956*
UK: ATLANTIC 781456-2
The Black Saint And The Sinner Lady *1963*
UK: IMPULSE! MCAD-5649
US: MCA MCAD-5649

MJQ
Django *1953, 1954, 1955*
US: PRESTIGE OJCCD-057-2
Last Concert *1974*
GERMANY: WEA INTERNATIONAL

781976-2
MJQ40: The Boxed Set *1952-88*
US: ATLANTIC 82330-2
The Artistry of the Modern Jazz Quartet *1952-5*
US: PRESTIGE FC D-60016

THELONIOUS MONK
At Town Hall *1959*
UK: RIVERSIDE OJCCD-135-2
US: ORIGINAL JAZZ CLASSICS CL OJCCD-135-2
Best Of Thelonious Monk (The Blue Note Years) *1947-52*
UK: BLUENOTE BNZ-261
US: BLUENOTE B21Y-95636
Blue Monk Vol 2
1952-4
UK: PRESTIGE CDJZD 009
Brilliant Corners
1956
UK: PRESTIGE OJCCD-026-2
US: RIVERSIDE OJCCD-026-2
Complete Riverside Recordings (15 CDs) *1955-60*
US: RIVERSIDE 15RCD-022-2
Live At The Five Spot Discovery! Featuring John Coltrane *1957*
UK: BLUE NOTE 0777 7 99786 2 5
US: BLUE NOTE 0777 7 99786 2 5
Misterioso *1958*
US: RIVERSIDE OJCCD-206-2
Monk's Music *1957*
UK: CARRÈRE 98948

US: ORIGINAL JAZZ CLASSICS CL OJCCD—084-2
The Unique Thelonious Monk *1956*
US: RIVERSIDE OJCCD-064
Thelonious Himself *1957*
US: ORIGINAL JAZZ CLASSICS CL OJCCD-254-2
Thelonious In Action *1958*
US: ORIGINAL JAZZ CLASSICS CL OJCCD-103-2
Thelonious Monk *1952-4*
US: ORIGINAL JAZZ CLASSICS OJC 010
Thelonious Monk With John Coltrane *1957*
US: ORIGINAL JAZZ CLASSICS CL OJCCD-059-2
Thelonious Monk With Sonny Rollins *1953-4*
US: ORIGINAL JAZZ CLASSICS CL OJCCD-059-2

JELLY ROLL MORTON
Complete Victor Recordings *1926-39*
UK: BLUEBIRD ND 82361
Library of Congress Recordings *1938*
UK: AFFINITY CD AFS 1010-3

GERRY MULLIGAN
California Concerts Vol 1 *1954*
UK: EMI CZ-65

California Concerts Vol 2 *1954*
UK: EMI CZ-67
Compact Jazz: Gerry Mulligan *1955-66*
UK: POLYGRAM 8306972
Compact Jazz: Gerry Mulligan Concert Band *1960*
UK: VERVE 838933-2
Lonesome Boulevard *1989*
UK: POLYGRAM 3953262
Mulligan Meets Monk *1957*
US: ORIGINAL JAZZ CLASSICS CL OJCCD-301-2
Pleyel Concert *1954*
US: VOGUE VG-600028
Reunion (With Chet Baker)
1957
UK: EMI CZ-52
The Best of the Gerry Mulligan Quartet with Chet Baker *1952-7*
US: BLUE NOTE CZ-416
US: BLUE NOTE B21Y-9548?

DAVID MURRAY
Ballads *1988*
US: DIW 840
Deep River *1988*
US: DIW 830
Spirituals *1988*
US: DIW 841

FATS NAVARRO
At The Royal Roost *1948*
UK: JAZZ VIEW COD-025

Fats Navarro
Memorial 1946-7
UK: SAVOY JAZZ VG-650150
Nostalgia 1946-7
UK: SAVOY JAZZ SV-0123
Roost Sessions 1948
UK: FRESH SOUNDS FSRCD-171

JIMMIE NOONE
The Complete Recordings Vol 1
1926-30
UK: AFFINITY AFS 1027-3 3CD

ANITA O'DAY
Anita O'Day Sings
The Most 1957
UK: POLYGRAM 829577-2
Anita O'Day Sings
The Winners 1958
UK: VERVE 837939-2
Anita O'Day Sings
Cole Porter 1952-59
UK: VERVE 849266-2
Compact Jazz Anita
O'Day 1952-62
UK: POLYGRAM 517954-2
Uptown (With
The Gene Krupa
Orchestra)
1941-9
US: COLUMBIA 45448

Sugar Foot Stomp
1926-31
UK: AFFINITY AFS 1025-2 2CD

KING OLIVER
Complete Vocalion/
Brunswick
Recordings
1926-31
UK: AMERICAN DECCA
GRP-1616-2
US: GRP GRD-616

**ORIGINAL DIXIELAND
JAZZ BAND**
75th Anniversary
Album 1917-21
US: BLUEBIRD 61098

KID ORY
Kid Ory's Creole
Jazz Band 1954
US: GOOD TIME JAZZ 12008
The Legendary Kid
1955
US: GOOD TIME JAZZ
GTCD-12016-2

CHARLIE PARKER
Bird: Complete
Verve Recordings
1946-54
US: VERVE 837141 (10 CDs)
Charlie Parker
Memorial Vol 1 1947
UK: SAVOY JAZZ SV 0101
Charlie Parker
Memorial Vol 2 1947
US: SAVOY JAZZ SV 0102
Charlie Parker
Memorial Vol 3 1947
UK: SAVOY JAZZ SV 0103
Charlie Parker:
Compact Jazz
1946-54
UK: POLYGRAM 833288-2
Charlie Parker:
Legendary Dial
Masters Vol 1
1945-7
US: STASH ST CD 23

Legendary Dial
Masters Vol 2
1945-7
US: STASH ST CD 25
Savoy Recordings:
The Master Takes
1945-8
US: SAVOY JAZZ ZD-70737

ART PEPPER
Art Pepper And
Eleven Modern Jazz
Classics 1959
US: ORIGINAL JAZZ CLASSICS
OJCD 341-2
Gettin' Together
1960
US: ORIGINAL JAZZ CLASSICS
OJCD 169-2
Intensity 1960
UK: FANTASY OJCD387-2
Meets The Rhythm
Section 1957
US: BORICITY CDCOP-004
Modern Art 1956-7
US: BLUE NOTE B21Y-46848
Smack Up 1960
US: ORIGINAL JAZZ CLASSICS
OJCD 176-2
The Art Of Pepper
1957
UK: BLUE NOTE BNZ-120

OSCAR PETERSON
Compact Jazz: Oscar
Peterson Plays Jazz
Standards
1964-6
UK: POLYGRAM 830698-2

Compact/Walkman
Jazz: Oscar Peterson
with Friends
1951-62
UK: VERVE 835315-2
Exclusively For My
Friends (4 CDs)
1963-8
UK: MPS 513 830-2
Night Train 1962
UK: POLYGRAM 821724-2
Very Tall (With
Milt Jackson) 1961
UK: VERVE 827821
We Get Requests
1964
UK: BLUEBIRD 810047-2

BUD POWELL
Compact Jazz: Bud
Powell 1949-56
UK: POLYGRAM CD 517995-2
The Amazing Bud
Powell Vol 1
1951-3
UK: BLUE NOTE BNZ-207
The Amazing Bud
Powell Vol 3
1956
UK: BLUE NOTE BNZ-173
The Best Of Bud
Powell (The Blue
Note Years)
1949-58
US: BLUE NOTE B793204-2
The Genius Of Bud
Powell 1950-1
US: POLYGRAM 827901-2
Time Waits: The
Amazing Bud
Powell Vol 4 1958
UK: BLUE NOTE BNZ-76

DJANGO REINHARDT
Swing in Paris
1936-40
UK: AFFINITY CDAFS-1003-5

BUDDY RICH
Compact Jazz:
Buddy Rich 1955-61
UK: POLYGRAM 833295-2
Illusion 1946-71
UK: SEQUEL NXT CD 181
Time Being 1971-2
UK: BLUEBIRD 64459-2

MAX ROACH
Deeds Not Words
1958
US: ORIGINAL JAZZ CLASSICS
OJCD-304-2

SONNY ROLLINS
A Night At The
Village Vanguard
Vol 1 1957
UK: BLUE NOTE BNZ 79
A Night At The
Village Vanguard
Vol 2 1957
UK: BLUE NOTE BNZ 81
Freedom Suite 1958
UK: GIANTS OF JAZZ
CD801213
On Impulse! 1965
UK: MCA MCAD-82496
Saxophone Colossus
1956
US: IMPULSE MCAD-5655

US: PRESTIGE OJCCD-291-2
The Quartets 1962
US: BLUEBIRD ND-85643
Way Out West 1957
US: BOPLICITY CDCOP-006
US: ORIGINAL JAZZ CLASSICS OJCD-337-2

JIMMY ROWLES
Remember When 1988
UK: MASTERMIX CHCHE-11

GEORGE RUSSELL
Ezz-thetics 1961
US: ORIGINAL JAZZ CLASSICS OJCD 070-2
Jazz Workshop 1956
UK: BLUEBIRD ND-86467
US: BLUEBIRD 6467-2
The Stratus Seekers 1962
US: ORIGINAL JAZZ CLASSICS OJCD-365-2

PEE WEE RUSSELL
Jack Teagarden/Pee Wee Russell 1938
UK: ORIGINAL JAZZ CLASSICS
Jazz Reunion 1961
US: CANDID CS 9020
US: CANDID CS 79020
Over The Rainbow 1958–65
UK: XANADU 192
Portrait of Pee Wee 1958
UK: CHARLEY CDFSCD-126
We're In The Money 1953–4

UK: BLACK LION BLCD 760909
US: BLACK LION BLCD 760909

DAVID SANBORN
Gil Evans: Priestess 1977
US: POLYGRAM 826770-2

ARTIE SHAW
Begin the Beguine 1938–41
UK: BLUEBIRD ND 90628
Blues In The Night 1941–5
UK: BLUEBIRD ND-82432
US: BLUEBIRD 2432-2
Last Recordings 1954
US: MUSIC MASTERS 65071-2
The Complete Gramercy Five Sessions 1940–5
UK: BLUEBIRD ND-87637
US: BLUEBIRD 7637-2

ARCHIE SHEPP
Fire Music 1965
US: MCA MCAD-39121

WAYNE SHORTER
Ju Ju 1964
UK: BLUE NOTE BNZ-85
Night Dreamer 1964
UK: BLUE NOTE BNZ-87
US: BLUE NOTE B21Y84173
Speak No Evil 1964
UK: BLUE NOTE BNZ-86

HORACE SILVER
Best Of Horace Silver Vol 2 1953–6
UK: BLUE NOTE 793206-2

Blowin' The Blues Away 1959
UK: BLUE NOTE BNZ-89
Cape Verdean Blues 1965
UK: BLUE NOTE BNZ-229
Six Pieces Of Silver 1956
UK: BLUE NOTE BNZ-175
Song For My Father 1964
UK: BLUE NOTE BNZ-200
The Jody Grind 1966
UK: BLUE NOTE BNZ-283
US: BLUE NOTEB21Y-84250

ZOOT SIMS
Blues For Two 1982
US: ORIGINAL JAZZ CLASSICS OJCD 635-2
Down Home 1960
UK: CHARLY CDCHARLY 59
For Lacy Day 1978
US: PABLO 2310942
If I'm Lucky 1977
US: ORIGINAL JAZZ CLASSICS OJCD 683-2
Just Friends 1978
US: ORIGINAL JAZZ CLASSICS OJCD 499
Warm Tenor 1978
US: PABLO 2310831
Zoot Sims And The Gershwin Brothers 1975
US: ORIGINAL JAZZ CLASSICS OJCCD 444
Zcot 1956
US: ORIGINAL JAZZ CLASSICS OJCD 228-2

BESSIE SMITH
Complete Recordings Vol 1 1923–4
US: SONY MUSIC 47091
Complete Recordings Vol 2 1924–5
UK: CBS 4687572
US: SONY MUSIC 47471

ART TATUM
Classic Early Solos 1934–7
UK: GRP GRD-607
US: GRP GRD-607
Complete Capitol Recordings Vol 1 1952
UK: CAPITOL 792866-2
US: CAPITOL C21Y-92866
Complete Capitol Recordings Vol 2 1952
UK: CAPITOL 792867-2
US: CAPITOL C21Y-92867
Solo Masterpieces Vols 1–8 1953–6
US: PABLO 2405432-2405439
Standard Transcriptions 1935–43
UK: MUSIC & ARTS CD-673
US:MUSIC/ARTS 673
The Tatum Group Masterpieces Vol 1 1954
US: PABLO 2405424
The Tatum Group Masterpieces Vol 2 1955

US: PABLO 2405432
The Tatum Group Masterpieces Vol 3 1955
US: PABLO 2405434
The Tatum Group Masterpieces Vol 4 1955
US: PABLO 2405435
The Tatum Group Masterpieces Vol 5 1955
US: PABLO 2405436
The Tatum Group Masterpieces Vol 6 1956
US: PABLO CD33J-20036
US: PABLO 2405430
The Tatum Group Masterpieces Vol 7 1956
US: PABLO CD33J-20034
US: PABLO 2405430
The Tatum Group Masterpieces Vol 8 1956
UK: PABLO CD33J-20034
US: PABLO 2405431
The V-Discs 1944–6
US: BLACK LION 760114

CECIL TAYLOR
Air 1961
US: CANDID 79046
Cell Walk for Celeste 1961
US: CANDID 79034
US: CANDID 79034
Jazz Advance 1956
UK: BLUE NOTE BNZ-281
US: BLUE NOTE B21Y-84462

Jumpin' Punkins
1961
UK: CANDID 79013
US: CANDID 79013

Looking Ahead 1958
US: ORIGINAL JAZZ CLASSICS OJCCD-452-2

New York City R&B
1961
UK: CANDID 79017
US: CANDID 79017

The World Of Cecil Taylor 1960
UK: CANDID CCD-90006

JACK TEAGARDEN

One Hundred Years From Today 1931-4
US: GRUDGE 4523-2

That's A Serious Thing 1928-57
UK: RCA BLUEBIRD ND 90440
US: RCA BLUEBIRD ND 9986-2

CLARK TERRY

In Orbit 1958
US: ORIGINAL JAZZ CLASSICS OJCCD-302-2

Power of Positive Swinging 1965
UK: MAINSTREAM MDCD-902

Squeeze Me 1989
US: CHIAROSCURO 309

MEL TORMÉ

An Elegant Evening (With George Shearing) 1985
US: CONCORD JAZZ CCD-4294

An Evening With George Shearing And Mel Tormé 1982

Compact Jazz: Mel Tormé 1958-61
UK: VERVE 833282-2

Lulu's Back in Town 1956
UK: CD CHARLY 5

Top Drawer 1983
US: CONCORD JAZZ CCD-4219

McCOY TYNER

The Real McCoy 1967
UK: BLUE NOTE BNZ-100

Today And Tomorrow 1963-4
US: GRP GRD-106
UK: GRP GRD-106

SARAH VAUGHAN

After Hours 1961
UK: ROULETTE CZ-235

Compact Jazz: Sarah Vaughan 1954-67
UK: POLYGRAM 830699-2

Compact Jazz: Sarah Vaughan Live 1957-63
UK: POLYGRAM 832572-2

Crazy And Mixed Up 1982
UK: PABLO CD 20043

How Long Has This Been Going On? 1978
US: PABLO 2310-821

The Divine Sarah Vaughan: The Columbia Years 1949-53
US: CBS 465597-2
UK: COLUMBIA 441165

JOE VENUTI

Joe Venuti And Eddie Lang 1926-33
US: DRG 36200

Joe Venuti And Eddie Lang: Jazz Classics 1926-33

Ben Webster And Coleman Hawkins 1926-33
UK: BBC BBCCD 644

Joe Venuti/Zoot Sims 1974-5
US: CHIAROSCURO 142

Violin Jazz 1927-34
US: YAZOO 1062

FATS WALLER

Fats And His Buddies 1927-9
UK: BLUEBIRD ND 90649

Fats Waller And His Rhythm 1934-6
UK: BBC BBCCD 684

Jazz Classics Vol 5: Fats Waller 1927-34
UK: BBC BBCCD-598

The Joint Is Jumpin' 1929-43
UK: BLUEBIRD ND 86288
US: BLUEBIRD 6288-2

The Last Years 1940-3
UK: RCA 61005-2

BEN WEBSTER

At The Renaissance 1960
UK: FANTASY OJCCD -3902

Ben Webster And Associates 1959
US: POLYGRAM 835254-2

Ben Webster And Coleman Hawkins
US: POLYGRAM 835254-2

Compact Jazz 1953-9
UK: POLYGRAM 833296-2

Ben Webster Meets Oscar Peterson 1959
3801062

See You At The Fair 1964
UK: IMPULSE! GRP 11212

The Tatum Group Masterpieces Vol 8 1956
US: GRP GRD-611

Count Basie: The Complete American Decca Recordings
1937-9
UK: PABLO CD0331-20034

TEDDY WILSON

Blues For Thomas Fats Waller 1974
US: BLACK LION 760131

Isn't It Romantic 1944-6
US: MUSICRAFT MVSCD-59

The Chronological Teddy Wilson 1939
UK: JAZZ CLASSICS-571

With Billie in Mind 1972
US: CHIAROSCURO 111

Here's To My Lady 1988
UK: CHESKY JD 3

Phil And Quill 1957
US: ORIGINAL JAZZ CLASSICS CL OJC 215.2

LESTER YOUNG

Charlie Christian And Lester Young: Together 1940
US: ARCHIVES OF JAZZ 3801062

Count Basie: The Complete American Decca Recordings
1937-9
UK: MCA GRP3-611-2
US: GRP GRD-611

Essence 1965-9
UK: SAVOY JAZZ ZD-70819

Jammin' With Lester 1946
UK: ARCHIVES OF JAZZ 3801182

Pres And Teddy 1956
US: POLYGRAM 831270

The Quintessential Billie Holiday Vol 4 1937
UK: COLUMBIA 463333-2

The Quintessential Billie Holiday Vol 5 1937-8
UK: COLUMBIA JAZZ MASTERPIECES 465190
US: COLUMBIA 44423

Walkman Jazz/with the Piano giants 1946-56
UK: VERVE 835316-2

PHIL WOODS

Flash 1989
UK: CONCORD JAZZ CCD-4408

index

acknowledgements

Photographs reproduced by kind permission of London Features International; Redferns/William Gottlieb, Max Jones, Andrew Putler, David Redfern, Gert Schlip, Chuck Stewart.

Front jacket: Rex Features.
Back jacket: Rex Features; Retna/Jay Blakesberg; Pictorial Press; Pictorial Press/Keuntje; Retna/Michael Putland.